WARSHIPS
AND WARSHIP MODELLING

WARSHIPS
AND WARSHIP MODELLING

David Wooley and William Clarke

Special Interest Model Books

Special Interest Model Books Ltd.
P.O. Box 327
Poole
Dorset
BH15 2RG

© Special Interest Model Books Ltd. 2006

ISBN 1-85486-405
EAN 978 185486 240 2

www.specialinterestmodelbooks.co.uk

Contents

INTRODUCTION   8

Chapter 1   **THE WARSHIP**   11
Design and Development • Classification of warship types •
Modern warships.

Chapter 2   **CONSTRUCTORS MODELS**   45
The Constructors Model • How they were made and why • Types of
warship models built by and for the shipbuilding industry •
The amateur model warship builder.

Chapter 3   **RESEARCH, PLANS AND HELPFUL PUBLICATIONS**   59
Research techniques • How to select information on specific ships •
Searching for and understanding plans • Key publications that will
be most helpful to the modeller • Photo Archives.

Chapter 4   **GETTING THE BEST FROM A WORKSHOP OR WORK AREA**   67
Planning a workspace • Managing the workspace • Providing for
adequate storage • Displaying of plans and associated materials.

Chapter 5   **THE CHOICE OF SUBJECT AND CONSTRUCTIONAL METHODS** 71
Choosing a subject • Selection of scales • Searching for the right
GRP hull Types and methods of construction • Preparation of GRP
hulls • Methods of scratch-building a hull.

Chapter 6   **INTERNAL FITTING OUT**   85
Planning and fitting out • Installing the drive train • Rudders and
rudder linkages, R/C, motors their selection and installation •
Power supply and installation methods • Test sailing and trimming
• Preparation for the deck and superstructure.

Chapter 7   **TECHNIQUES FOR BUILDING OF WEATHER DECKS**   95
AND SUPERSTRUCTURES.
Techniques for building up superstructures • Bridge areas, Turrets,
masts • Selection of materials • Understanding adhesives and
bonding agents.

Chapter 8   **FITTINGS, ETCHED WORK AND CASTINGS**   111
Warship Fittings, old and new • Ships boats • Constructing single
item fittings, multiple fittings and resin castings • Commercial
fittings, selection and preparation • Etched brass fittings • Fitting
etched stanchions, making railings from scratch, deck planking •
Making aircraft from scratch • Radar arrays • Ships fittings general.

Chapter 9   **PAINTING AND CAMOUFLAGE**   141
Preparation, selection of paints, type of finishes, camouflage,
application.

Chapter 10   **PREPARATION AND OPERATION OF**   153
WORKING MODEL WARSHIPS
Methods of Ballasting, R/C equipment • General maintenance •
Presentation for shows and exhibitions • Steering techniques.

APPENDIX 1 – GLOSSARY OF TERMS   167

APPENDIX 2 – SOURCES OF INFORMATION   168

APPENDIX 3 – SPECIALIST MANUFACTURERS   170
           AND SUPPLIERS

REFERENCES   171

Foreword

David Wooley and William Clarke have made an important contribution to ship-model building with this edition of *Warships and Warship Modeling*. Readers will find that the authors use a somewhat different approach to the topic than found in most other books on model building.

Unlike the usual format, Wooley and Clarke's book begins with a large selection of excellent photographs of actual ships that will help the model builder choose a subject for a future endeavor or better visualize a current project goal. Numerous close-aboard shots of these ships offer excellent detail that will help the model maker plan a project and determine the level of complexity he wants to pursue, whether in a static display or an operating model.

Whatever the project, a model represents a sizable commitment in time and personal resources. The authors have provided an authoritative guide that enables the modeler to make the most of both from concept to completion. As the book progresses, the reader is taken through all of the steps necessary to build a first-class model, including researching plans and photographs, workshop essentials, methods of hull and superstructure construction, fittings, painting and finishing, displaying, and more.

A book of this nature is a considerable undertaking that would usually be attempted only by an experienced model maker and seasoned researcher. Both authors are ideally suited to the task. Their experience, commitment to their subject, and extensive resources are evident throughout. Although obviously a presentation for the model maker, naval historians and enthusiasts also will find this work appealing on many levels, to be read from cover-to-cover or used as a spot reference.

The appendices contain a wealth of information. They list most of the museums, archives, and related repositories in the United Kingdom, Europe, and the United States. In addition, there are sources for plans, photographs, building supplies, and specialized tools for the modeler.

Warships and Warship Modeling will be a valuable and extremely useful addition to the library of every modeler, whether a professional, seasoned, or novice builder, as well as historians and others fascinated by ships of war.

Robert F. Sumrall
Assistant Director and Curator of Ship Models, Retired
United States Naval Academy Museum

Introduction

Currently there are a number of books published exploring and defining the methods and techniques available for the study and building of model warships. This is a favourable situation as it allows for a useful pool of knowledge on the subject that can be accessed as and when the need arises.

However there are few that have approached this subject from a perspective that draws the reader directly from the prototype to the model via a view of the methods used by the industry that built this type of ship.

The primary aim of this book is to lead the reader from an "industrial" view of ship models into an altogether different dimension but connected by a common thread. These parallel worlds of model warship building are peopled on the one hand by the enthusiast or accomplished amateur, and on the other in the ship building industry; those that provide equipment and services.

In the latter, models are built that are seldom seen in museum galleries or builders' trade exhibitions, yet achieve a level of competence that can almost be the full size vessel in miniature. These models frequently inspire the viewing modeller or would-be-modeller to go on to realise their potential and follow their passion to build a working or static model warship.

A further aim in the leading chapter is to provide a guide through the definitions of various types of warships. There are many acronyms and type designation abbreviations used in this and subsequent chapters that are expanded in the Appendices to avoid regularly breaking the flow of the text.

In the process the reader will be helped to appreciate, through first rate photographs, (many of which have remained unpublished up until now) the form and function of the warship not just as a vessel of war but as a statement, and in a few instances, an embodiment of national pride.

Constructors models or those built on the instructions of the builder or the client have been part of the "Industry" for generations. Perhaps today not having the same importance as in the past, but remain a way of graphically illustrating in small scale what the designer and builder are endeavouring to achieve or have achieved.

Museums are still a major resource for the study and understanding of the model warship and by their very presence an appreciation of the prototype. Sadly a large number of these models remain out of reach for those with a casual interest in the subject and are housed in storage facilities often separated from the museum proper. Some undergo conservation to enable future generations to appreciate the shape and form of the warships that shaped our history, but often this task is overwhelming and financially burdensome to a point where many such artefacts are neglected and as such can deteriorate beyond the point of recovery.

It is in the second chapter that attention is focussed on this form of model, which in the age of electronic 3D graphics remains something more tangible, almost a link with the original ship, that no electronic medium can duplicate.

Although, as will be discussed at length in Chapter 2 builders' models from past generations were in many respects an overt almost garish presentation of the builder's product and not an altogether "true replica" of the prototype. Yet their very presence can, on the one hand be an inspiration to the modeller, and on the other, provide source of genuine interest for the naval historian, enthusiast, general public, young and old alike.

The aim of the following chapters is to help translate the

desire and possible inspiration gained to make that transition from passive enthusiast with an interest in warships to active modeller and help to give guidance down a more practical path. At this point to give the reader an insight into the process of research, understanding the value and application of plans and the use photographic material as pertains to individual ships.

Here chapters relating to the development of a workshop or modelling area with practical help and tips on how to utilise space, and the tools and equipment required. Whilst at the same time thoughts are focusing on the type of constructional methods available.

Once all these decisions have been made further chapters will help guide the reader through the various stages of construction from preparation of the hull, to fitting out the power train, radio control equipment requirements and installation , Adhesives and bonding agents, materials, methods required for building superstructures and fittings.

Approaches to preparation of commercial items such as resin and white metal fittings, cold moulding processes. The use of photo etch

The closing chapters concentrating on preparation for finishing, methods of paint application with brief references to weathering and camouflage. The final chapter focuses on the requirements for preparation of the completed model for water and ultimately the joy sailing the new creation that is a model warship.

Chapter One

The Warship

This book, which is essentially focused on the model warship, retains as its central theme that link that has always existed between the model and the prototype. Thus the opening chapter deals almost exclusively with the prototype from the early stages of construction to launch and ultimately to the form that best illustrates the meaning of the word Warship. This appraisal is intended as a general overview of the warship and its type.

It's neither an anthology nor a practical lesson in shipbuilding but more an examination of the rationale, function and form of the prototype. The reader may be disappointed that their "favourite" or their choice of ship that might be best suited to illustrate the word warship is not included but inevitably a selection of images had to be made.

Many of the images however, are more representative and are not placed in any official chronological order or in any rigid historical context. A number of those shown could be considered as the "ultimate" expression of type for example the "Des Moines" class cruiser or the "Arleigh Burke" class DDG. It is the aim of this chapter to give some insight into the meaning of the word "Warship" through the inclusion of a number of exceptional photographs. Many of these have not been included in any other publication and should inspire the reader to appreciate both the function and form of these great ships.

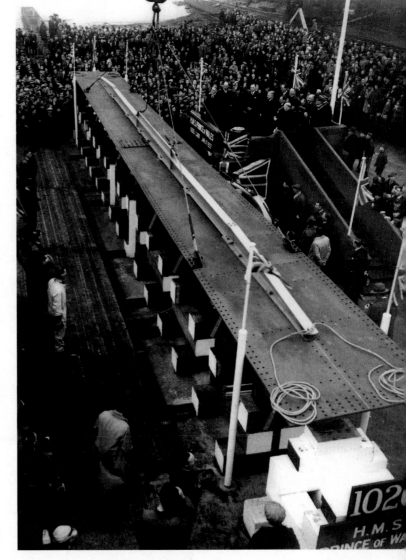

Photo 1 Keel laying ceremony for the British battleship HMS Prince of Wales at Cammel Lairds shipyard Birkenhead. *(Photo Wirral Archive Service)*

The beginning

Traditionally ships, and in particular warships have begun their life on a building slip, an example of which can be seen in **Photo 1**. Until now very little has been mentioned in books devoted to model building of how a warship traditionally took form during its initial stages of construction. Many of the ships featured in this chapter were built using what can be described as traditional methods and were constructed on a single site by a single shipyard.

Building methods and requirements have changed dramatically over the last 50 or so years and very few warships are built from the keel up on a single slip today.

Warships today are as often as not built in sections or sub-assemblies by a number of contractors with each of the dedicated sections constructed in large building halls. Here new technologies are employed and robotic equipment used and instead of the thousands employed to construct a single vessel, this figure has now reduced to a fraction of that traditional work force. These assemblies are taken perhaps miles from their site of build and reassembled, with a precision that many acquainted with traditional methods would find hard to understand.

Equally the methods of preparation have changed completely since the introduction of computer technologies. Drawing offices were large complexes housing many hundreds of skilled draughtsmen, where many hundreds if not thousands of differing sets of drawings were prepared for every aspect of the ships construction.

With the advent of 3D CAD (Computer Aided Design) traditional methods of draughting changed beyond recognition and now planners can provide up to date "spatial" computer models, comprising many thousands of individual components where fast and easy data exchange is commonplace. The information generated can, without expensive outlay and preparation, be transferred from the design stage to production. An example of this form of advanced high precision warship manufacture can be appreciated in **Photo 1** (see colour section). Here components are first cut, machined and formed to the required shapes before being transferred to large assembly halls, where the sub-sections and their services are fitted into place ready to be transferred to the slip for final assembly.

The slip as seen in **Photo 1** shows the keel laying ceremony for the battleship HMS Prince of Wales and is typical of the area where a vessel would be built from the keel up. Engineered into the base is a slope, part of which would be above the water line and part below. On this surface was placed what are termed "land ties". Lengths of timber usually at 6-7ft spacing into which concrete is levelled. This in turn provides anchorage for all the subsequent timberwork.

Groundways

Groundways are sections of timber, usually fir and generally 12in square, that are laid on the land ties in such a manner that the weight of the hull would be sufficient to overcome the initial friction of the ways, and surprisingly, that of the water, in the later stages of launch. The spread of the ways depends on the type of vessel being built and it is usually considered to be one third the beam of the ship. It was also considered standard practice in the days when vessels were built entirely on the slip, to lay out groundways of sufficient width apart that hulls of varying sizes could be accommodated.

The traditional method used for building on the ways required the assembly of many professions, trades, skills and vast quantities of material, whose joint efforts resulted in the skeletal form rise up from the building blocks, to ultimately take on the more familiar shape we have come to appreciate as the warship in all its guises.

Launching

Generally it was common practice, soon after the outer bottom compartments had been tested as being watertight, for work to begin on the "cradle". This was part of the support for the launch and was constructed on either side of the hull just abaft of the bow. The cradle would be released from the hull soon after launch usually assisted by a tug.

The actual time of launch is decided upon some weeks prior to launch day and is tide dependent. Usually the ship is prepared 24 hours before and on the day the final stages of setting up are completed. Setting up usually involves the weight of the vessel being transferred from the building blocks to the groundways. In order to maintain momentum down the slip, the groundways are well greased with a melted down mix of tallow applied usually a few weeks before launch. Prior to launch the ship is made watertight by closing down the hatches and watertight doors.

As the ship is about to be launched, all remaining blocks under the fore end are knocked away along with other various procedures for releasing the cradle from the slip. The vessel should then begin to slide with increasing momentum down the slip. In certain circumstances hydraulic rams are employed to overcome any initial resistance. Part way down the slip, as the hull enters the water, the moment of buoyancy will become equal to the moment of weight at the bow. This is graphically illustrated in the photograph of the launch of HMS Prince of Wales on the April 3rd 1939. **Photo 3**. At this position the stern lifts and will continue to lift until finally buoyancy equals weight and the ship is completely water borne.

Once the ship is fully launched the momentum has to be arrested. This is sometimes achieved by dropping anchors but more usually by the fitting "drag" chains sited on either side of the slip.

With the launch successfully completed, the ship is towed into the fitting-out basin. Here the remainder of the superstructure, machinery, guns and general services are built in and provided for.

The warship and the model

Individual photo files or "walk abouts" on various ships presented in Chapter1 are included here. These consist largely of the exterior and where the need arises, relevant parts of the interior of the ship, with as much information on the structure of the vessel as possible. A good example is how, in the USN one class of ship, the cruiser, has evolved from the closing stages of WW2 through to the advent of the missile age and how the present term cruiser is defined.

Complementing this general overview pertaining to the full size vessel, a number of photographs of models similar to the warships featured have been included to illustrate how effective the working models of the same or similar vessels can be made to appear.

There are parallels when embarking on building of a model to that of the full size ship. The construction of a model can be organised in a way that allows the model to be built in orderly stages that interrelate with each other: from construction of the hull, installation of hardware, superstructure and fittings. However this relationship often begins with and is helped by some basic understanding of the full-size counterpart.

Classification of the warship

Generally classification of various warships from the immediate post war period has become more ambiguous; for example the word "frigate" can define a warship of moderate size of say 2,000 tons to almost 10,000 tons, nuclear powered and well armed. Although the nuclear powered frigate has now passed into history, the role of a frigate as an escort, has remained fairly constant since 1945.

Equally the cruiser has changed markedly since 1945. Many that evolved during the Cold War have actually reduced in displacement when compared to more traditional so called heavy cruisers and were developed almost exclusively around the missile, either for air defence, anti-ship or land attack.

The Carrier CV, CVN

The aircraft carrier has also changed from the conventionally powered "Essex" class CVs of the immediate post war period, through to the larger 79,000 ton "Forrestal" class of the mid 1950s, to the emerging of the CVN or nuclear powered, super carrier in the 1960s. The first of these behemoths, the USS Enterprise at 1,123 ft long still retains its position as the longest carrier ever built.

By contrast the Royal Navy at the end of WW2 had no less than 11 carriers in commission and even increased these numbers marginally in the early 1950s. But with constant fiscal constraints this figure was to decrease markedly over the following years, culminating in the scrapping of the last remaining "fixed wing" aircraft carrier HMS Ark Royal in late 1978. These were to be replaced by three "through

deck cruisers", a political euphemism for the word carrier, being re-designated as CVH, ASW carriers in 1980. Unlike carriers possessed by the USN, the 20,000 ton 677ft length "Invincible" class could only support a small mix of VTOL strike aircraft and helicopters having a very different role to that of their USN counterparts. Similar but larger vessels of the Soviet "Kiev" class entered service with the Soviet navy in the late 1970s supporting (as with the "Invincible" class) a limited number of VTOL aircraft and ASW helicopters.

The Battleship - BB

The word battleship derives its place from the age of sail via the "ship of the line of battle". Although battleships in modern terminology, are seen as warships having guns of large calibre that can be fired from revolving turrets and fitted with substantial amounts of armour. The basic concept of which started in the 1858 with the building the French frigate la Gloire designed by Dupey de Lome and completed in 1860, followed closely by the Warrior, often attributed with being the first representation of such a class of ship. By the turn of the 19th century the basic tenets of the term "battleship" were well established.

Unlike many of the classes of ships outlined here, by the close of WW2 the battleship, as a type was very much in decline. Britain and France continued to complete such ships post WW2. For example HMS Vanguard was completed in 1946. Although the French battleship Jean Bart was launched in March 1940 it was not until January 1949 that her sea trials were undertaken. Only the USN was to retain the battleship as a principle weapons platform throughout the period of the cold war either in reserve or activated. Iowa BB61 and the Wisconsin BB64 remain officially in reserve.

Destroyers - DD, DDG

The destroyer from the immediate post war period, evolved to meet the changing needs of first, the Cold War (particularly in the areas of ASW and AAW), then to conditions in the post Cold War environment of anti ballistic missile defence as well as retaining the more traditional role of AAW. Once again the definition of the word destroyer became blurred. The USN retained much of its wartime fleet into the post war period and these vessels were subsequently included in FRAM (Fleet Rehabilitation and Modernisation) upgrade programs. Newer DDs such as the 5,000 ton Forest Sherman and particularly the "Tarter" armed Charles F Adams and the "Terrier" armed "Farragut" class of ASW escorts were completed in the 1960s at the height of the Cold War.

These were supplemented by DLGN or nuclear powered destroyers; Bainbridge and Truxtun later to be re-classified as fleet escort cruisers or CGNs. British development post war concentrated more on ASW to counter the growing Soviet submarine threat and, as a stop gap interim measure, converted many existing hulls and re-designated these as ASW frigates. Equally the single largest, USN conventional destroyer was the 9,200 ton "Spruance" and "Kidd" class. These were fitted with ASROC missiles for anti submarine defence, "Sea Sparrows" for air defence and later units in the class, mounted the Mk 41 VLS "Tomahawk" and "Harpoon" anti-ship missile whilst still retaining their DD prefix (see Appendix 1 for ship classification).

Whereas the "Arleigh Burke" class are classified as DDGs they are presently sub-divided into Flight 1, 2 and 2As and are not quite as large as the "Spruance" class, but like the "Ticonderoga" class of CGs, are equipped with the "Aegis" air defence system. The RN still retains a small number of Type 42s, "Sea Dart" equipped DDGs soon to be augmented by the first of a new generation of DDGs, the Type 45s.

The Frigate - FF, FFGs

As stated, the modern concept of the term "frigate" really began in the period following WW2 when the major naval threat was perceived to be the Soviet submarine force. This was based on the intelligence that the Soviets were using advanced German technology gained from the type XXI and XXIII U-boats.

To meet this threat the British converted many of its older wartime "emergency" destroyers into ASW frigates. To this end much of the original superstructure and weapons fit

was removed. This was replaced with a new all-aluminium superstructure including fully enclosed bridge and a limited gun fit of 2x 4in/45calibre. These were controversially mounted aft supported by 2, 40mm Bofors guns. This armament was supplemented with the all-important Type 170 sonar and initially two "Squid" mortars aft, later replaced by the much more effective "Limbo" Mk10. This type of "new ships for old" doctrine was at the time, in the years of post war austerity highly successful and politically acceptable.

Post-war design of frigates, at least in the RN, concentrated on ASW. This was later reinforced by the 1,535 ton Type 15 or "Blackwoods"class that were considered a rather basic design when compared to the larger Type 12s with the lead ship of this class, HMS Whitby, being laid down in September of 1952. Unlike the Type 15s, the "Whitby" class saw the reinstating of twin 4.5in/45 guns in a single mounting which was the weapon of choice right through to the "Leander" class. A flight deck and hanger for the ASW "Wasp" helicopter was retro fitted to the "Rothesay" class of Type 12s.

Both the Type 15s and 12s were geared, steam turbine powered. However diesels were introduced for the first time

Photo 5 A stunning 1:144 working scale model of CVN-68 USS Nimitz

Photo 7 CVE-122 the escort carrier
USS Palau *(Photo Nobe Smith)*

Photo 9 BB-57 USS South Dakota

(U.S. National Archives)

Photo 10 The French Battleship Richelieu on the 11th February 1943. New York City harbour entrance. *(U.S. National Archive)*

in a post war design in the following Type 41/61 "Leopard" and "Salisbury" classes of AA frigates. Originally fitted with long range Type 960 air warning radar, eventually both classes were to receive the AKE-1 965 air warning system.

The Type 12 hull design, with its characteristic raised forecastle and rounded deck edges, was repeated with modifications on the highly successful "Leander" design that mounted a long-range early warning radar and the effective "Limbo" ASW mortar and exhibited improved sea keeping qualities.

Later re-fits show the removal of the forward 4.5in gun in favour of the "Ikara" GW40, a rocket assisted homing torpedo. A further eight in this class were converted to operate "Exocet" MM38 missiles mounted forward.

British frigate design evolved further in the 1970s with the introduction of the COGOG a dual gas turbine propulsion system. First installed in the controversial 3,600 ton Type 21s, a design built on the margins, with no capacity for future upgrades in weapons systems. The class had an effective performance and armed with MM38 and "Sea Cat" missiles, made for an effective FFG.

The follow-on Batch 1 Type 22s were intended to act as

leader of an AS task force and combined with the ASW carriers were to form a highly mobile and powerful ASW battle group. Apart from "Exocet", the Type 22s at 4,400 tons for the batch 1s and 4,900 tons for the batch 3s of the "Cornwall" class, were fitted with 2x 6cell box launchers for "Sea Wolf" close-range missile system sited both fore and aft. For ASW, the STWS-1 TT for the Mk 46 or "Stingray" torpedoes.

In the early 1980s design work began on the Type 23 design or "Duke" class. A major departure from the previous 22s in so much as the machinery was CODLAG, a combination of gas turbine and diesel electric, which makes for almost silent running when deploying a towed array. Although slightly smaller than the 22s, the Type 23s are fitted with multiple launch "Sea Wolf" VLS and "Harpoon" SSM.

In the USN the introduction of the FF and FFG was more protracted although by definition the need for dedicated ASW ships became evident soon after the end of WW2. Like the RN, the USN inherited large numbers of existing destroyer hulls. Principally amongst these were the "Fletcher" and "Gearing" classes, which were converted to carry "Hedgehog" and later "Weapon Alpha", an early ASW rocket mortar. As with the British experience, these DDs with their geared turbine propulsion machinery, produced the speeds required to engage the perceived Soviet submarine threat. Yet, unlike the RN, the USN did not designate these ASW ships as frigates but adopted the description of "Ocean Escorts" or DDEs and later ships DEs.

The first of the post war escorts was the 1,877 ton "Dealey" class. These single screw DEs were fitted with 4x3in/50 calibre guns, all but one of the class received "Weapon Alpha" forward of the bridge and the SQS-4 sonar. The follow-on classes are discussed later in this chapter. However it was not until mid 1975 that the category of DE was dropped in favour of FF and FFG, perhaps reflecting the emergence of the new missile-armed frigate capable of functioning in AAW and ASW.

Carriers

When considering a choice of subject to model, there are a number of factors that will need consideration. Whilst many of the criteria surrounding such a choice will be discussed in subsequent chapters, it is worth relating here some of the more basic tenets. Certainly one of the main elements that will influence that decision is personal choice. This followed by scale, which will have a direct bearing on the eventual size of the model, which in turn affects handling and transport.

Harry S Truman - CVN 75

Take for example the mean measurement of the flight deck on the 1088x257ft 6in super carrier Harry S Truman CVN 75 **Photo 4** (see colour section). Even at a modest scale of 1:144, the model would be over 7ft long and 28in in beam. Subsequently applying the same formula for 1:100 scale (see

Chapter 5) the same model would increase proportionally to a not so manageable size of over 10ft in length with a maximum beam of 31in. However at these scales there is a huge scope for fine detailing especially with the inclusion of the air wing, which brings such a model to life.

Ted Parr's super detailed CVN68 - USS Nimitz

Although built to a relatively modest scale of 1:144, a model such as a super carrier can be packed with fine detail, a good example of this is in Ted Parr's truly impressive working model of the USS Nimitz seen here in **Photo 5**. Even the crew are dressed in the appropriate coloured shirts. **Photo 6** (see colour section)

USS Palau - CVE122

A further subject popular with modellers is the CVE. Even at a scale of 1:96 a manageable sized model can be built. **Photo 7** shows the USS Palau (CVE122) of the "Commencement Bay" class. Interestingly, on the flight deck are "ASW Avengers" and abaft of the island structure a twin rotor helicopter HUP. This is quite unusual and indicates a post war deployment, possibly Korea in the early 1950s with the picture dated January 8th 1953.

HMS Invincible - CVH (RO5)

A further variation on the carrier theme is this striking photo of HMS Invincible embarking the "Harrier" F2A-GR7, "Sea King" and "Merlin" helicopters seen here refuelling from the Royal Fleet Auxiliary replenishment vessel Fort Victoria. **Photo 8** (see colour section).

Although relatively small by carrier standards, these "support carriers" have proved their worth over many years and have undergone a number of refits. The most recent being the removal of the large Type 909 radar-housing forward of the bridge and the "Sea Dart" air defence missile system forward, with the cable deck being plated over providing additional deck space.

The Battleship - USS South Dakota BB57

The battleship is a popular subject for the model maker and one such design that typifies that general interest is the USS South Dakota seen here in **Photo 9**. Official photographs are almost always dated, so references can be very precise and ideal for the modeller.

The South Dakota BB57 was lead ship of this 35,000ton class along with Indiana BB58, Massachusetts BB59 and the Alabama BB60. All of the class were equipped with 16in/

Photo 12 Looking towards the forecastle of the French Battleship Richelieu. Note the series of 20mm mountings abaft of the breakwater. *(U.S. National Archives)*

Photo 11 The catapult and hanger replaced by quad 40mm Bofors on Richelieu. *(U.S. National Archives)*

Photo 13 Richelieu from the forecastle looking aft *(U.S. National Archives).*

Photo 14 Richelieu on the starboard side looking up towards the armoured tower *(U.S. National Archives)*.

Photo 15 This picture has plenty of detail for the modeller – Richelieu *(U.S. National Archives)*.

Photo 16 Richelieu – boat stowage arrangement *(U.S. National Archives)*.

Photo 17 Richelieu looking aft from atop of the triple 152mm mounting *(U.S. National Archives)*.

Photo 18 Richelieu adjacent to the after cable holder looking forward towards triple 152mm turrets. Note the 20mm mountings marked "6" on the photo (*U.S. National Archives*).

45calibre Mk 6 guns in a 3x3 turret arrangement plus 20x5in 38calibre Mk 32, DPs in a 10x2 arrangement (16x5in South Dakota only). This, on a relatively short hull of 680ft length overall when compared with the preceding "North Carolina" class at 729ft length overall or the "Iowa" class at 887ft length overall.

On 21st August 1942 the South Dakota received no less than 16, 40mm and 20, 20mm quad mounted guns making the battleship an ideal AAW platform to accompany the fast carriers. This was confirmed on the 26th of October when in concert with the carrier USS Enterprise she was attacked by no less than 45 Japanese aircraft. In response, South Dakota's 40mm and 5in DPs downed no less than 26 aircraft..

Battleship Richelieu

Two of the most striking warships of their genre of the period 1940-1956 were the French battleships Richelieu and Jean Bart.

Richelieu was extensively photographed when undergoing a major re-fit in the New York navy yard between February 11th and August 3rd 1943 and the photographs presented in this publication are amongst some of the most detailed photos of Richelieu ever recorded in her wartime configuration.

This 47,500 ton battleship shared a number of common features with the earlier British battleships Nelson and Rodney in mounting all of their main armament forward.

In Richelieu this required the 8x380mm/45calibre guns to be mounted in a 4x2 arrangement similar to that adopted by the earlier "fast battleships" (31.5 knots) of the "Dunkerque" class.

Under the requirements of the 1935 program three battle ships of the "Richelieu" class were to be built, Richelieu, Jean Bart and the Clemenceau with both Richelieu and Clemenceau being built at Brest dockyard. Only Richelieu was near to completion before the fall of France in June 1940. Apart from the 8x380mm, the secondary armament consisted of 9x152mm/55 calibre guns in a 3x3 arrangement. These were augmented by 12, 100mm/45calibre in a 6x2 configuration. Plus 12, 37mm (6x2) and 24, 13.2mm (6x4).

Importantly a large hanger and two catapults for three Loire "Nieuport" 130 floatplanes was sited aft on the quarterdeck.

At 47,500 tons performance provided by the 179,000shp Parsons 4 shaft, geared turbines was at a fast 32.5 knots, which was an improvement over the preceding "fast battleships"

Photo 19 Richelieu re-fitted *(Photo U.S. National Archives)*

Photo 20 CVA-73 USS St Paul as in April 1959. *(Photo Nobe Smith)*

Photo 21 "Des Moines" class heavy cruiser USS Salem August 1958 *(Photo Nobe Smith)*

Dunkerque and Strasbourg.

Photo 22 The Soviet gun cruiser "Sverdlov".

With the fall of France in June 1940 and the subsequent armistice, Richelieu was ordered to Dakar in French North Africa and in the port of Oran on 3rd of July 1940 all French naval forces received an ultimatum to submit to one of a series of British demands. With the French refusal to comply came the British response. On the 3rd of July the French Fleet at Oran was subjected to a stand-off bombardment by Admiral Somerville's battleships including the battle cruiser Hood and a follow up torpedo bomber attack on the July 6th. On the morning of the 7th an attack was mounted on Dakar by six "Swordfish" torpedo bombers from the carrier Hermes. One torpedo was said to have struck Richelieu under the stern causing severe structural damage around the stern casing and inner starboard shaft. On 23rd of September, although badly damaged, Richelieu's guns helped thwart an attempt by Anglo-Free French forces to mount an invasion of Dakar.

Richelieu was to remain at Dakar throughout 1940-41 and into 1942 and it wasn't until November of 1942 that the situation in North Africa, and by implication, the fate of the battleship Richelieu was to change. Following the Invasion of North Africa in late 1942, it was accepted by the Vichy French forces that all French naval forces including the Richelieu were to be allied with the Anglo/US/Free French forces.

Thus on January 23rd 1943 Richelieu, was taken in hand and successfully moved to the United States for a total overhaul and upgrade, **Photo 10**. The re-fit even involved the re-bore of the 380mm gun barrels to accommodate the British 381mm rounds. Apart from the major task of repairing the torpedo damage, which involved the re-aligning of the shaft, there was a re-working of the AA fit. This called for the installation of no less than 50, 20mm Oerlikon and 67, 40 mm Bofors, in 11 single and 14 quad mountings. Amongst the most noticeable structural changes was the removal of the hanger and catapults aft, **Photo 11**.

The following series of photos show the Richelieu in her post re-fit configuration. Up forward in **Photo 12** and immediately abaft of the break water are a row of 20mm Oerlikon mountings with **Photo 13** showing the same position looking from the cable holders forward. Note also the inclusion of the large blast bags surrounding the barrels. Photographs of this quality can be great value to any model maker with a desire to build Richelieu and see the changes this ship underwent in 1943. As a matter of interest there are references to "fighting lights" numbered 14-15 on the photo, these are in fact a series of coloured lights, which are an optical recognition system.

Moving further aft on the starboard side in **Photo 14** there is a view of the armoured tower and bridge from a position adjacent to the forward 380mm turret. Although Richelieu had undergone a re-fit which involved major structural changes, a large percentage of the superstructure remained "as built" therefore still useful to any model maker intending to build a model in the original configuration.

For example many of the original fittings remain in place. These include mundane items as WT doors, hand rails, ladders and the photos show how many of the structural components relate to other parts of the main superstructure, **Photo 15** is a good example. Looking up towards the up-take note the grill on the underside of the casing and the quad 40mm marked "4" in the photo. A similar situation exists in **Photo 16**, which shows the new arrangement of the ships launches forward of the main mast from that of the original design to permit a more effective distribution of the smaller calibre AA guns. This photo also gives an opportunity for the modeller to see the supports for the ships boats in more detail, which is not always possible.

The final three photos relating to Richelieu focus on the after section, which was considerably altered in the 1943 re-fit. Here the off-set catapults, crane and hanger facilities have been removed and replaced by 16, 40mm Bofors in a 4x4 arrangement which can be seen clearly in **Photo 17**. Adjacent to each mounting is the director tub and in the position of the hanger are 9, 20mm guns. Note the 20mm mountings atop of the after 152mm turret marked "6" in **Photo 18**.

Apart from being given a more effective camouflage scheme, Richelieu was now a far better defended warship with regard to air defence; thus a very useful asset. From March 1944 until May 1945, except for a very brief visit to Toulon in October of 1944, Richelieu was actively involved in operations in the Indian Ocean and the Far East being temporarily assigned to TF57. Following the cessation of hostilities in August 1945 this symbol of French sea power was to remain in service for a further 22 years until she was removed from active service in late 1967 being disposed of the following year, **Photo 19**.

Cruisers CA, CG, CGN

By the end of WW2 the battleship had been relegated to No.2 in the hierarchy of warship classes and was approaching the end of its evolutionary cycle. The USN by contrast had embraced the concept of the cruiser in to the post war years and beyond. It is therefore the intention of this chapter to bring to the fore just a small number of cruiser designs that can be considered to have crossed the threshold from the age of the gun to the dawn of the missile age. These vessels transformed the way navies fight and defend their airspace. Also included is a design that caused considerable unease when it first appeared in the early 1950s.

The two most numerous designs for cruisers possessing 6 and 8in guns, the "Cleveland" and "Baltimore" classes, were emerging as the war in Europe was about to start.

The "Cleveland" class were essentially "post treaty" cruisers developed from the original concept of an 8,000 ton ship armed with 6in guns to a vessel of over 14,000 tons fully loaded armed with 12x6inch guns. The secondary armament

Photo 24 CAG-2 gun/missile combination as fitted to the USS Canberra. *(Photo Nobe Smith)*

consisted of 12x5in guns in a 6x2 arrangement and a 28, 40mm AA fit. Although based on the "Helena" design and dogged by stability problems more "Cleveland" class were built than any other class of cruiser but few saw service following the end of WW2.

However the following "Baltimore" class were altogether a more stable design. At 13,700 tons, they were 54ft longer than the "Clevelands" (610ft) at 664ft but more importantly the beam was increased from 66ft 4in on the "Clevelands" to nearly 71ft.

Unlike the 6in main armament fitted to the "Clevelands" the larger "Baltimores" received the 8in/55 calibre guns, plus a secondary fit of 12, 5in/38calibre guns, augmented by an AA complement of 48, 40mm guns. Following the end of WW2 those "Baltimores" that survived the reduction in numbers underwent modifications. These were to include the replacing of the 40mm mountings with ten 3in/50 calibre guns seen here on the USS St Paul in the late 1940s to early 1950s, **Photo 20**.

Apart from the commissioning of "Worcester" and "Roanoke" in 1947 no other 6in gunned cruisers were completed after WW2. With the USS Oregon City (CA122) and Rochester (CA124) entering service in early 1946. "Fargos" were 6", single stack "Clevelands", they were considered equivalent to the "Fargo" class and in many respects a precursor to the largest and probably the most powerful conventionally armed heavy cruiser ever built. "Oregon City" and "Rochester" were 8" single stack "Baltimores" and do not compare with "Fargos".

The Des Moines

The Des Moines, Salem and Newport News displaced 21,500 tons with a hull length of 716 ft 6in loa by 76ft 6in beam and were all completed between January 1948 and January 1949. Interestingly "Des Moines", although completed with catapults and crane, never actually embarked floatplanes. The main armament being the 8in/55 calibre, as per the "Baltimores", was in effect a new weapon that had an automatic reloading system. This provided for the first time, a high volume of fire at 20RPM (Rounds Per Minute) and an integrated round using brass cartridges that could be loaded at any angle.

The "Des Moines" could be considered the ultimate "gun" cruisers and were actually larger than a number of battleships. Such a formidable gun system came at a cost and this was measured in the increase in weight for both the hull and turrets. **Photo 21** shows USS Salem as she appeared on

August 9th 1958 fitted with the 10, 3in/50calibre guns. The 3in/50 right forward was removed in the 1950s as being too exposed (wet). The radar fit consisted of the SPS6B air search, SG6 surface search unit at the masthead, plus an SR2 air search.

The Soviet "Sverdlov" class

No sooner had WWII finished than the Soviets saw the emerging power struggle with the West as inevitable and a struggle that would be conducted on many levels. Stalin considered the possession of a "blue water" navy as just one of the instruments in that struggle to project Soviet military and political influence. Thus the one single naval asset that could contribute to this political doctrine with a clear strategic aim, was the "Sverdlov" class of gun cruisers, the last of this type post-war.

Sverdlov was laid down at the Baltic yard, Leningrad, on October 15th 1949 and commissioned on May 15th 1952.

Photo 28 USS Long Beach exposing the SPG 49 Talos missile tracking radars mounted on the after superstructure *(Photo Nobe Smith)*.

Photo 29 A 1:96 scale model of the Long Beach seen at "Santee" regatta California. *(Photo Kurt Grainer)*

Sverdlov - the model

This 1:96 model of the Sverdlov successfully captures the classic lines of the Soviet era cruiser. The model is scratch built using the plank on frame method of construction (see Chapter 5) and measures over 2m in length. All of the superstructure is built up using litho plate (thin metal) plastic and timber with many of the fittings, ships boats and 100mm/57 mountings cast from a master mould in resin. The entire model took approximately two years to build. **Photo 23** (see colour section).

Entering the missile age

Interestingly for the modeller, and perhaps not always appreciated, the move over to adoption of the missile for warship armament produced, at least in the early years, a mix of old and new technologies with a number of striking if not controversial conversions. These, in a modelling context, would be quite a challenge. Most of this post-war development took place aboard ships of the USN.

There was a series of factors that induced the seismic shift in the offensive/defensive capability of the surface warship. Essentially the lessons of WW2 were still very much to the fore, particularly the use of German guided weapons and the Japanese suicide pilots both of which were very difficult to stop using conventional gun armament and as a result had a devastating effect both materially and on morale.

In response the USN needed a system that was both fast and accurate. This gave rise to "Project Bumblebee" a wartime initiative to produce surface to air guided weapons Although the results of this project did not arrive in time for the closing stages of WW2 the seeds were sown for what was to become the USN's first generation of guided weapons systems; principally the long-range ramjet assisted "Talos" and the shorter-range rocket propelled "Terrier" missile systems. Both of which made use of "beam riding" command guidance.

The British beam riding equivalent to "Talos", was "Sea Slug" using the Type 901 target tracking radar installed in the purpose-built guided missile destroyers of the "Devonshire" class. For the USN the platform of choice had to be one of a large number of cruiser hulls available post war, as a completely new design from the keel up was not politically or economically acceptable in the early years following the end of WW2.

There were a number of permutations in missile/hull configuration, which seem quite bizarre from our 21st century perspective but then seen as a feasible alternative. For example, the German V2 rocket installed as an early "ballistic missile" in hulls ranging from the suspended "Iowa" class Kentucky to the suspended "Alaska" hull of the Hawaii.

Originally there were to be 24 ships in the class but only 14 were completed. At 17,500 tons 210 meters in length by 20m in beam, they were similar in displacement and proportions to contemporary USN designs. Fitted with steam turbines developing 110,000shp driving two shafts with a maximum predicted performance of 32 knots (Sverdlov actually attained 33.5knots).

Photo 22, shows Sverdlov in the late 1950s exhibiting lines with a tinge of Italian influence. Yet, unlike the "Baltimore" class of USN cruisers as mentioned previously in this chapter, the "Sverdlovs" resembled more the "Clevelands" in fire power but having 12, 152mm/57 calibre main armament in a 4 turret arrangement, similar to those fitted to the preceding "Chapaev" class.

Also included were 12, 100mm/50 calibre DP guns which perhaps look strangely familiar having some close similarities to the German 105mm. For close AA defence Sverdlov was fitted with 32, 37mm semi-automatic twin mountings. Unlike the contemporary post war Des Moines, the "Sverdlov" class were designed without any form of aircraft catapult.

Although entering service as gun cruisers, the Soviets like the USN, saw the potential of the cruiser hull for the installation of missiles. The Admiral Nikhimov was probably the first of the class (if not the first Soviet surface warship) to be fitted with guided weapons. This was followed by the Derzhinsky having a single SA-N-2 (Surface to Air Missile) twin-armed launcher sited aft replacing the "X" turret. Whilst the Zhdanov was to have the SA-N-4 and along with the Senyavin were converted to so called "command cruisers" in 1972, and as such had facilities for operating helicopters. The Murmansk was the last of the Sverdlov class to be decommissioned in 1992.

Photo 32 opposite top DD-864 USS Harold J Ellison *(Photo Nobe Smith)*

Photo 33 opposite DDG-940 USS Manly "Forrest Sherman" class.

CAG-2 - USS Canberra

Eventually the first warships to become missile capable were the "Baltimore" class cruisers USS Boston and Canberra. These 17,947 ton cruisers were large enough but a hybrid compromise was decided upon whereby the forward 2x3, 8in gun turrets were retained along with 10, 5in and 8, 3in/50s in a 4x2 arrangement. Whilst the after section accommodated two launchers in "X" and "Y" positions. These had a magazine capacity of 72 missiles per launcher for the "Terrier/Talos" missiles using the large SPQ-5 guidance radar mounted forward of the launchers seen here on USS Canberra, **Photo 24**. Interestingly other structural changes involved the trunking the 2 funnels into a single stack. A new pole mast supporting the CXRX hemispherical scan radar for use with the "Terrier" directional radar was also installed.

USS Boston (CAG1) entered service as a "missile armed fleet escort cruiser" on the November 1st 1955 joined by Canberra (CAG2) on June 5th 1956. As a matter of interest, Boston was completed with two additional 3in/50s sited on the main deck abaft of the 5in/38s. A further modification, certainly reflecting the uncertainty of the period, was an NBC wash down system (now a common feature on most warships).

From a modelmakers perspective, these two vessels would make attractive subjects using the "Baltimore" hull form. Equally the challenging aspects for any build would be the tall lattice fore mast and the CXRX search radar plus the SPS-6 air search radar mounted atop of the foremast and aft of the tall pole mast, the SPS-29 air search radar. Strangely, but perhaps reflecting the obsolescence of these two ground breaking cruisers, they were once again to become CAs with the removal of the missile launchers. However the useful days were numbered, Boston was struck off the register in November 1973 and Canberra in July 1978.

In their way these two ships represented a leap in technology such as that heralded by the advent of the Dreadnought but the real test was yet to come.

All missile ships – "Albany" class

USS Albany, Oregon City and Rochester began as part of the "Oregon City" class and in their original appearance were very much akin to the super cruisers of the "Des Moines" class. These ships represented a leap of faith from the

Photo 34 Missile armed DDG-19 USS Tattnall Charles F Adams class. *(Photo Nobe Smith)*

Photo 35 First of the class DDG-51 USS Arleigh Burke June 1991
(*Photo Nobe Smith*)

Photo 36 A 1:96 scale model of the USS Barry.

conventional concept of a cruiser to the revolutionary all-missile armed warship and sported an appearance to match. Very few ships have undergone such a level of transformation. The 18,700 ton Albany at 647ft long by 71ft beam, underwent modernisation at the Boston navy yard between January 1959 and November 1962. The original superstructure to the main deck was re-built with the then unusual combination of high mast and stack and missile launchers fore and aft supporting "Talos" (with the smaller "Tartar" launchers mounted either side of the superstructure forward).

Due to genuine concerns over the basic vulnerability to attack by FAC boats and low-flying aircraft, of these "missile" ships, two 5in/38calibre guns were retro-fitted soon after completion mainly due to the insistence of the then president John F Kennedy.

Once again from a modeller's perspective these ships were anything but ordinary and would make a real challenge as a modelling subject. Unusual they are, ugly and ungainly they may be, but as a model they would seldom be ignored.

The first of the nuclear navy - CGN USS Long Beach
The nuclear philosophy for surface ships took hold in 1955, with the USS Long Beach first of a new generation

of nuclear powered all missile armed warships laid down in December of 1957. Although using a hull similar in many respects to the "Baltimore" design the Long Beach represented the "Dreadnought" of her age. Revolutionary in armament, propulsion and radar. Initially intended as a nuclear "frigate" displacing 16,606 tons in a hull 721ft 3in length by 73ft 3in beam, she was at that time the first cruiser designed and constructed from the keel up for the USN since the end of WW2. She was propelled by two pressurised water-cooled reactors driving two geared turbines producing 80,000shp.

The single feature which dominated the entire profile, was the SPS 32/33 fixed array liquid cooled, electronically scanned search radar, capable of detecting aircraft out to an astonishing range, (for the period) of 300nm. Each of the four so called "bill board" SPS 32 panels surrounding the box shaped bridge/superstructure, were 40x20ft with an all-up weight just short of 80 tons. Supported by the same box superstructure was the companion SPS 33 25x20ft panel, tracking radar of **Photo 26**. The only other surface warship to receive the SPS32/33 was carrier USS Enterprise pictured here with "Skyraiders" on the flight deck on October 24th 1962, **Photo 27**.

Long Beach was fitted with 2 twin-arm Mk10 launchers forward for the short range "Terrier" SAM missile and, forward of the bridge, the two SPG 55 "Terrier" fire control radars. Aft is a single twin-launcher for the larger, long range "Talos" missiles. On the aft superstructure are mounted the two huge SPG49 "Talos" tracking radars incorporating microwave lenses seen here in April of 1963, **Photo 28**. Like the "Albany" class, Long Beach was to be retro-fitted with two single 5in guns amidships abaft of the ASROC launcher.

Interestingly, on a tour of duty off Vietnam in 1968, Long Beach was credited with downing two Mig 19s at a range of 65nm. The "Talos" missile systaem was removed in 1980 followed in 1982 by the SPS32/33 radar array, due in part to the high maintenance cost. The SPS49 air search and SPS48 3D radar replaced this in turn. Long Beach had the longest service career of all the nuclear cruisers. Serving from September 1961 until being decommissioned in July 1994. In a modelling context Long Beach makes for an interesting subject and is seen here in her original configuration to a scale of 1:96 and being put through its paces at a regatta at Santee California, **Photo 29**.

CGN-38 - USS Virginia

There was a proposal for the inclusion of "Aegis" and the SPY-1 phased array radar into the "Virginia" class of DLGNs subsequently to be re-defined in 1975 as air defence cruisers and prefixed CGNs. Note the Mk 26 launchers fore and aft for the "Tartar" standard SAM (Surface to Air Missile) which eliminated the need for separate ASROC launchers **Photo 30** (see colour section). The photo shows CGN-38 equipped with Tomahawk box launchers right aft.

Photo 37 bottom Graceful lines of the stretched Type 42 DDG HMS Manchester.

Photo 38 below right Knox class USS Ainsworth with raised forecastle *(Photo Nobe Smith)*.

Photo 39 above right Flush forecastle "Knox" class DE-1085 USS Donald B Beary *(Photo Nobe Smith)*.

The Aegis cruiser - "Ticonderoga" class

The concept of the Aegis cruiser has its origins in the 1960s passing through the possibility of such a system being used in the nuclear cruiser programme of CGNs and the proposed "strike cruiser", until eventually being installed in the conventionally powered CG47 cruiser project of the "Ticonderoga" class. Design work as such began in the early 1970s and classified as DDGs later to be re-classified to CGs.

The class was to be made up of 27 ships with the lead ship Ticonderoga entering service in January 1983 (now decommissioned) and the final ship CG73 USS Port Royal being commissioned April 30th 1994. The defined role is AAW or air defence of the battle group against aircraft and anti-ship missiles, whilst retaining an effective ASW role.

USS Chosin - CG65

The photographed example of this first generation "Aegis" ship is CG65 USS Chosin and at 9,900 tons in a hull of 563ft length by 55ft beam, is relatively small by cruiser standards of the past and this even represents a slight ambiguity of class when compared to the DDG 51s at 9,400 tons.

Originally the first 5 in the class CG47 to CG51 were fitted with 2 twin Mk 26 (MOD1) launchers for 88 "Standard SM2" MR missiles. From CG52 onwards VLS is fitted in 61 cell clusters fore and aft. This is clearly visible in **Photo 31** (see colour section) depicting CG65 USS Chosin, note also the

Photo 41 FFG-31 Guided missile armed frigate USS Stark *(Photo Nobe Smith).*

Photo 42 right above Nuclear powered "frigate" USS Truxton *(Photo Nobe Smith).*

Photo 43 right below Attack transport "APA 136 USS Botetourt. *(Photo Nobe Smith).*

127mm/54 calibre Mk45 gun aft. Yet this gun whilst designated DP has no AA capability. The two dishes surmounting the aft superstructure abaft of the main mast are SPG60 radar illuminators for the "Aegis" system, with a further SPG60 forward atop of the bridge.

The core of the whole air defence system is the SPY-1 phased array radar. The individual octagonal panels associated with the system are also clearly visible in the photo, with two sited on the after superstructure to port and aft. Whilst the forward SPY-1 panels face to starboard and forward. As a matter of interest each antenna contains 4,480 separate elements and covers a 90degree quadrant from the horizon to zenith enabling a 360degree scan out to a range of 200nm.

Destroyers DDs to DDGs - DD864, USS Harold J Ellison

Following the end of WW2 a major re-think was underway as to what type of destroyer was required. In the immediate

post war years the USN had at its disposal large numbers of wartime constructed vessels. These included vessels of the later "Gearings" of which it could be said here that they were the best of their genre from that period incorporating many of the hard lessons learned from the Pacific war. Particularly replacing the 40mm guns with the 3in/50s. It was in these 3,479 ton 390ft destroyers that a number of the most far-reaching experiments were undertaken.

USS Witek, for example, was converted for use with pump jet drive whilst in 1956 the Gyatt was fitted with the "Terrier" missile becoming the very first DDG.

Photo 32 shows the Harold J Ellison fitted with ASROC amidships and a platform for DASH operations.

DD940 USS Manly - "Forrest Sherman" class
The "Forest Sherman" class had the distinction of being the largest conventionally armed destroyer of the early to mid 1950s at 4,050 tons and 418ft 6inches length by 45ft beam. In

this design there was a marked shift to air defence. Initially being fitted with 3 of the excellent 5in/54calibre guns and 4, 3in/50 calibre AA, plus "Hedgehog" ASW throwers. Later modifications, perhaps reflecting the role of "fleet escorts", involved the removal of one 5in replacing this with the ASROC ASW seen here aft on USS Manly **Photo 33** and the inclusion of the SQS 23-35 sonar's. Interestingly the USS Bigelow was the trials ship for the "Phalanx" CIWS whilst the hull provided a test bed for the lightweight 8in/55 calibre gun.

It was intended that all the class were to be fitted with a single launcher aft for the "Tartar" missile; however out of the 18 ships in the class only DD936 USS Decatur, DD932 John Paul Jones, DD949 Parsons and DD947 Somers were actually converted between 1965-68. Most were constructed at Bath Iron Works including the USS Manly, with the USS Parsons being the only one of the class to be built at Ingalls.

DDG19 USS Tattnall - "Charles F Adams" class
In many respects a larger version of the preceding "Forrest Sherman" class but unlike the "Forrest Shermans" were designated DDG or missile armed destroyer. In all 23 hulls

Photo 45 Amphibious Command Ship USS Mount Whitney. *(Photo Nobe Smith)*

Photo 46 USS Big Horn "T-AO 198" Replenishment oiler *(Photo Nobe Smith)*

were laid down between June 1958 and February 1962 with the lead ship Charles F Adams entering service in August 1960. The superstructure in common with the "Forrest Shermans" was built using aluminium in order to reduce weight particularly above the main deck.

Initially the first 8 in the class were to be all-gun ASW destroyers but were re-classified as DDGs before construction began and were fitted initially with the twin arm Mk11 launcher aft for 42 "Tartar" missiles. Later units were fitted with the more reliable Mk13 single arm launcher as seen in **Photo 34** of DDG19 USS Tattnal.

The "Charles F Adams" were larger than the "Forrest Shermans" and fitted for ASW with an 8 cell ASROC launcher amidships. Abaft of the after stack, and mounted one above the other, are two SPG 51C tracking and illuminating radars for the "Tartar" missile and the SPG 53 radar forward of the foremast for the 5in fire control. The photo shows Tattnal pre-modernisation, which included new ECM sonar and combat systems. Export versions were built for both Germany and Australia with the "Ikara" ASW system replacing ASROC.

USS Arleigh Burke - DDG 51, Flight 1

Certainly the "Arleigh Burke" class was one of the most significant designs of any destroyer initiated during the Cold War. Primarily an air defence destroyer and as such fitted with the powerful, SPY-1 "Aegis" phased array radar system incorporated as panels into the sides of the forward superstructure. This advanced design, with a high degree of radar reflective "stealth" surfaces, is complemented by an assortment of weapons, which include a 90 cell VLS SAM forward and aft, 8 anti-ship "Harpoon" missiles and a single 5in/54calibre forward, **Photo 35** (See Colour Section).

The design unlike any other has evolved considerably since the 1980s to meet the changing requirements of the 21st century, from the original DDG51 of 8,315 tons and 504ft 7in length by 67ft 11in beam through the Flight 2 variants and into the slightly lengthened Flight 2A's. Post DDG79 Flight 2A's are fitted with a dedicated hanger facility accommodating 2, SH60-R "Seahawks" plus an increase in space for 96 "Block IV" standard missiles and "Tomahawk" land attack missiles.

Although the 2A's are slightly longer and heavier at over 9,300 tons, there has been a reduction made in the weight of the upper superstructure. Fitted from DDG81 onwards the

5in/62 calibre, Model 4 naval gun is designed for use with ERGM and has a distinctive, low radar visible gun house.

Model of DDG52 - USS Barry

The hull of this 1:96 scale model of the USS Barry had been built on a GRP hull available in the USA from *Loyalhanna* and at the time when writing, the Flight 2A variant, from *Sirmar* in the UK. **Photo 36** shows the superb detail on the Barry by Paul Simpson. The superstructure made up from styrene sheet, with all of the fittings provided by *Sirmar*. The model is seen on its early trials and performs exceptionally well.

British DDG development

In a number of respects, British post-war destroyer development mirrored that of the USN with the prime function of the destroyer providing escort and support of the carrier task force. A significant number of laid up wartime destroyer hulls were also re-built and reclassified as ASW frigates to provide a credible ASW force in the face of the growing Soviet submarine threat.

Reflecting this parallel trend with the USN wartime destroyer construction, that included programs such as the "C" class, "Battle" class, "Weapons" class and the immediate post war "Daring", class were to provide the backbone of the post war destroyer force. Unlike the USN experience, there were no equivalents in the RN in the 1950s of the USS Gyatt DD712, a "Gearing" class destroyer converted to a DDG in April of 1957. It was not until the early 1960s that existing British destroyer were retro-fitted with the "Sea Cat" point defence missile system.

The first British DDG, HMS Devonshire, entered service in November 1962 and was equipped with "Sea Slug", a 19ft 8in beam-riding, long-range (26miles) surface to air missile. The "County" class, of which there were eight, displaced 6,800 tons and were 505ft long more akin to a light cruiser than a destroyer. Nonetheless they were handsome ships and when equipped with "Sea Cat" were the only British warship at that time to have a long and short range missile system. In 1972 further additions followed with the installation of the four box launchers forward of the MM38 "Exocet" anti-ship missile.

The following Type 82 class, laid down in November 1967, were intended as fleet escorts for the cancelled CVA-01 carrier program and as such only one of the intended four, HMS Bristol, was completed. However there was much that was new including the highly regarded "Sea Dart" missile system with its more efficient twin-arm launcher. Plus the all-new Vickers Mk8, 4.5/55calibre automatic, rapid-fire gun and the "Ikara" anti submarine rocket. Bristol was the only three-funnel warship since the "Abdiel" class of fast cruiser minelayers built in the early 1940s. And like the previous "County" class of DDGs, the Type 82 was COSAG powered.

The requirements for air defence at sea remained. Thus a smaller design, the Type 42, was initiated and the first of this all-new class HMS Sheffield was laid down at Barrow shipyard on January 15th 1970. Although lighter than the Type 82 by 3,350 tons and shorter by nearly 100ft, the Type 42 incorporated "Sea Dart", the Mk8, 4.5in gun and a spacious hangar.

DDG HMS Manchester - stretched Type 42

HMS Manchester, the first of the "stretched" or Batch 3 Type 42s entered service on December 16th 1982. Due to the accentuated lines of the lengthened hull form, the Batch 3s could be considered to be amongst the most attractive destroyers ever built. Essentially a 50ft longer version of both the Batch 1&2s but due to weight problems all the class were given additional strengthening strakes along the top of the hull amidships. Apart from the increase in size of the hull, the weapons fit remains the same as that currently fitted to the remaining Batch 2 Type 42s, **Photo 37** (see colour section).

DEs, DEGs and FFs

Basically the DE has the primary task of ASW, with a size and performance similar to the frigate as categorised in the British Navy. The first of the USN post war DE construction began with the small 1,877 ton "Dealey" class laid down in October 1952. (See USS Cromwell, **Photo 38**. Note for ASW "Weapon Alfa" is sited forward of the bridge). The following "Claud Jones" class of diesel powered DEs, possessed a rather modest performance of 21knots and fitted for ASW with the forward firing "Hedgehog" system, which was of limited value against the newer generation of Soviet submarines possessing higher underwater speeds.

Due in part to the limited performance and ASW weapons capability of the previous classes, the next class of DEs corrected some of these inherent deficiencies. The result was the "Bronstein" class, which were larger and reverted back to the use of geared turbine propulsion. Although they were a significant improvement on the rather disappointing "Claud Jones" class only two were ever constructed, Bronstein and McCloy. Unlike the previous DEs the "Bronsteins" were fitted with the trainable ASROC, ASW system plus the more efficient SQS-26 sonar array.

Certainly progress in providing useful ASW and AAW platforms gained momentum in the mid 1960s with the introduction of the ASROC equipped, 27knot Garcia and the "Tartar" missile equipped "Brooke" classes. Essentially the division of the class reflected weapon fits. Vessels from DE1040 to 1051 were ASW whilst the following DEG1 USS Brooke to DE6 were missile armed.

"Knox" class DEs

The "Knox" class were numerically the largest group of warships of destroyer escort type constructed to the same design. Although heavier and larger than the "Garcia/Brooke" class the "Knox's" in their "as built" configuration

Photo 38 USS Cromwell DE 1014. Note the ASW "Weapon Alpha" forward of the bridge.

were wet ships forward. To reduce this effect a bulwark was added to the forecastle and spray strakes added just abaft of the bow. **Photo 39** shows the Donald B Beary, DE1085 as originally built, whilst **Photo 40** USS Ainsworth, illustrates the changes forward.

Unlike the preceding "Garcia /Brooke" classes with a twin 5in/38 guns, the "Knox" class received a single 5in/54 which was considered a better choice. Equally the larger telescopic hanger facility, could accommodate the LAMPS1 helicopter increasing the ASW potential over the rather unreliable DASH drone and like the previous class, the "Knox" was fitted with ASROC. Air defence was improved between 1971 and 1975 when 31 of the class were fitted with the "Sea Sparrow" point defence missile system. Interestingly in 1975 the entire class were redesignated Frigates or FF and by 1983 "Phalanx" was replacing the "Sea Sparrow" for close-in weapon defence. Following the seismic changes in the early 1990s, initiated by the end of the Cold War, the "Knox" class were deemed surplus to requirements and many of the class were made available for transfer; both the Donald B Beary and Ainsworth went to Turkey in May 1994.

USS Stark - FFG31

By the autumn of 1976 the first of the "Oliver Hazard Perry" class had been launched and between November 1979 and August 1989, 51 of the "Perrys" entered service. Fitted with a single shaft and aluminium superstructure the original design was not without controversy. At over 4,000 tons the "Perry" class are substantial FFGs and larger than the preceding "Knox" class but fitted with an OTO "Malera" 76mm (3in/ 63calibre). Unlike the "Knox" the "Perry" design does not include ASROC but relies for ASW detection and attack on a combination of the SQR19 towed array sonar, two LAMPS helicopters and 6, Mk32 TT. For AAW, the class were fitted with the Mk13 single arm, MOD 4 missile launcher. The design however is flexible enough to allow further re-fits and extend their like well into the 21st Century, **Photo 41**.

CGN, DLGN and FF - USS Truxtun

Categorising is not a straightforward application as it first appears and can be confusing. A good example is how the "Knox" class was re-classified from a DE to FF or Frigate. However the converse is also true. A further example can be seen in the USS Truxtun **Photo 42**, a 540ft long, 8,927 ton nuclear powered fleet escort cruiser, equipped with a twin arm "Terrier" missile system and a single 5in/54calibre gun. In nomenclature terms, it is now known as a CGN but was also classed as a DLGN or nuclear powered destroyer. Yet like the USS Bainbridge was originally considered a nuclear powered, missile armed frigate. Confused? Well, ship types are occasionally re-classified upwards and downwards depending on the role they fulfil.

APA - USS Botetourt - Attack Transport

There are groups of specific warship types that can be classed as "amphibious assault ships", which were developed as such during WW2. **Photo 43** shows the "Attack Transport" USS Botetourt or APA 136. However since WW2 doctrines have changed and presently the prefix LPH refers to a vessel capable of transporting and inserting troops/marines by helicopter into a landing area beyond the beach. Where as the role of the APAs were to embark troop into landing craft and then to the beaches.

LPH - Landing Platform Helicopter HMS Ocean

Like the first USN LPHs, the British made use of converted carriers Bulwark and Albion in late 1950s and early 1960s. Although not a dedicated vessel, each ship was capable of lifting up to 800 marines using eight Helicopters. Whereas, the "Iwo Jima" class of LPHs for the USN, were the first of their type designed and built as "helicopter assault ships" retaining the carrier concept of a large expanse of flight deck but smaller than the converted "Essex" class and the British Bulwark and Albion.

Ocean is the RN's first LPH built from the keel up. Commissioned in 1998 and capable of lifting 500 marines and their equipment (with the aid of 12 "Sea King" HC4 helicopters), including vehicles and artillery, **Photo 44** (see colour section). They have, if the situation dictates, the capacity to transport up to 15 GR7, "Harrier" VTOL aircraft. Complementing the airlift capability are four LCVP, Mk 5 landing craft.

LHDs

Within the nomenclature of differing amphibious warfare ships are the LHDs. Essentially these are a vessel that can accommodate and launch (from a flooded internal dock), various forms of landing craft, LCVPs and LCACs, whilst having facilities for operating helicopters from a flight deck.

LCCs - USS Mount Whitney.

Both LCC19 USS Blue Ridge and LCC20 USS Mount Whitney were designed in the early 1960s as AGCs. Entering service in late 1970 and early 1971 respectively, although the present nomenclature remains in place, the role has changed slightly to Joint Command Craft JCC, equipped to carry three LCP and two LCVPs. Surprisingly for ships of 19,729 tons and 620ft length, both LCCs have only limited helicopter capability but as their primary task is command and control, both ships are fitted accordingly with a wide variety of systems and equipment. These include ACIS, NIPS and can provide such services as TACC and HDC to name but a few. Equipped (2006) with only a basic defence capacity which includes "Phalanx" 2x20mm plus 2 single, "Bushmaster" 25mm single mounts and 4, 12.7mm MGs. Both LCC19 and 20 are assigned as Fleet Flagships, **Photo 45**.

AO - USS Big Horn

No warship or fleet could move very far from home waters without replenishment at sea. For this task the USN has a large capability at its disposal. Each type of ship is given its own prefix denoting its task and all begin with "A". For example AOs are fleet oilers, AKS cargo ships, AFS combat store ships, ATS salvage and rescue and so on. Operation of these ships is either the responsibility of the USN or Military Sealift Command, which often have a combined crew of "civil service mariners" and Naval personnel or naval reserve forces.

Photo 46, USS Big Horn AO198 is a good example and forms part of a class of 16 TAOs all laid down between August 1984 and June 1992. The Big Horn is approximately 9,500 tons when light but this rises to 42,000 tons fully loaded and is fitted with 32 fuel oil tanks. Power is primarily diesel with a diesel-electric combination for slow running. Big Horn has five replenishment stations, 3 to port and 2 to starboard with a flight deck right aft but no hanger facility.

Chapter Two

Shipbuilders and commercially made models

The question can be put which came first the model or the real ship. For generations the model was the full size ship in miniature in the shape of Navy Board models. As the construction of ships changed so did the shipyard model. Following the building of the warships Nemesis and Phlegethon in 1839 by Lairds of Birkenhead, a new scientific approach to ship building was beginning to emerge based not on wood but first on iron then steel. The traditional use of the Navy board model was therefore to be replaced by tank test models and demonstration/display models.

The shipyard model

Warship models like any builder's model were commissioned at the request of a prospective client as part of the contract. Sometimes the builder would have two models made providing a scaled, often embellished representation of the original ship that was a valuable tool in demonstrating the builder's product. Either way these models were used to impress and at the same time demonstrate the latest design and to a certain extent this still holds true. Take for example this projected design of the new British CVF complete with air wing of JSF aircraft, seen at the Thales pavilion at the 2005 International Festival Of The Sea, **Photo 47**.

Photo 47 The proposed CVF carrier for the Royal Navy.

2.1 The superstructure on Vickers model of the IJN Kongo.
(Photo by kind permission Dock Museum Barrow)

Photo 2.2 14inch turret as fitted IJN Kongo. Note how the fittings are finished.
(Photo by kind permission Dock Museum Barrow)

Photo 1.1 Extract from a Basset Lowke catalogue circa 1930.

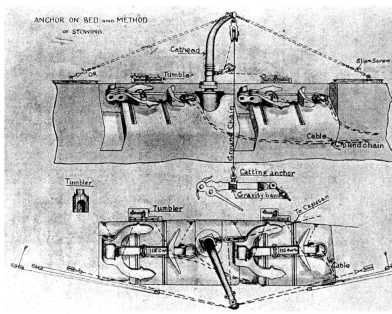

Fig. 3.1a How bed anchors are stowed.

Photo 3.1b Bed Anchor and its fittings.
(Photo by kind permission Dock Museum Barrow)

Photo 3.2c A "bow stopper" for holding the cable.
(Photo by kind permission Dock Museum Barrow)

A controversial ship, a controversial model

However ship builders models as such became more of a feature around the 1860s. Take for example this superbly crafted 1:48 scale 58in long model of the CSS Alabama currently on display at the Williamson art gallery, Birkenhead. **Photo 48** (see colour section). Although not conforming in all detail to the original, it remains a highly rated builder's model and only one of two such examples of the CSS Alabama in existence, the other being at the Mariners Museum Newport News. Andrew Bowcock in his book "CSS Alabama Anatomy of a Confederate Raider", makes the point that this model did not form part of the original "Lairds Model Room" collection and as such a question mark remains over its origins as a builders model. Interestingly though, its omission from that collection could of course be attributed more to the controversy and notoriety that surrounded the vessel following the end of the American Civil War, when the British Government had to pay compensation to the United States under the Alabama claims ruling. This may have reflected very negatively on the builder Lairds of Birkenhead.

Most builders' models are of course free from an impression of being "tainted goods". However, the days of the shipyard

3.3 Rigging arrangements on the main mast of the pre-dreadnought HMS Vengeance. *(Photo by kind permission Dock Museum Barrow)*

Fig.3.2 How a davit is rigged.

3.4 Typical davit arrangements for a cutter.
(Photo by kind permission Dock Museum Barrow)

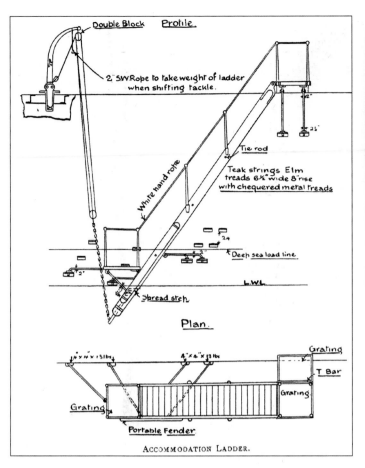

Fig. 3.5 General illustration as to how the ladder was secured.

3.6 A night life buoy was a common feature on many warships before and during WW1. *(Photo by kind permission of Museum of Transport, Glasgow)*

4.1 The open barbette of the battleship HMS Resolution. Note how the deckhouse windows and doors are presented *(Photo by kind permission of the Discovery Museum)*

model maker's shops are long gone but it was in these shops, some forming part of the joiners shop and within eyesight of the full-size vessel, that some of the finest warship models were produced. Only a few of the staff in the model shop were in fact trained as model makers, many came to the shop as joiners, cabinet makers or apprentices and used their skills perfecting models. Although to be fair not the entire model

5.1 Gibbs and Cox built USS Agerholm. *(Photo by Naval Sea Systems Command)*

was built in-house, many of the fittings were commissioned from a manufacturer specialising in model ship fittings.

The commercial model maker - Photo Series 1

One of the best known commercial model makers was Basset-Lowke, It is through their catalogue that you can take a glimpse into the past for not just the wide range of models but in the pricing of these models built for private collectors, ship owners and travel companies. Interestingly, in their 1930

3.5 Accommodation ladder as fitted to the IJN Hatsuse. *(Photo A Barlow)*

6.2 As with the Agerholm this LST model was used to evaluate the internal arrangement. *(Photo by Naval Sea Systems Command)*

catalogue, they illustrated a huge range of fittings for all types of models including warships; an example of this can be seen in **Photo 1.1**.

Many of the ships represented by builders' models have long gone but it is through the viewing of these models that we can gain an appreciation, not just of the ship represented, but the true skill of the model makers, whose ability and workmanship made these models possible. From a personal perspective it was as a young boy of eight that my father introduced me to this world of shipbuilding through the medium of models, even before I was introduced to the full-size vessel.

As stated, these models graced the boardrooms and entrances to many of the once famous shipyards in the United States and the UK. Few of these premises remain and fewer retain any of their prized model collections. Also, in years past, museums regularly displayed their model collections in an almost regimented way, with lines and lines of glass cases.

6.3 "Atlanta" class cruisers Juneau II CL-119.
(Photo by Naval Sea Systems Command)

However in recent years the shipyard-crafted model has been included in a number of specialised more thought-provoking displays. These are used to explain, particularly in areas were shipbuilding or trade was the main stay of the town and surrounding area, how these ships were built and the people involved in their construction. As part of this process the builders' models are used to graphically illustrate like no other medium can, the achievements of ordinary people in the construction and purpose of these great ships.

Presenting Builders' Models - Photo Series 2

One of the best examples of this new way of presenting models is within the Dock Museum at Barrow in Furness Cumbria (see Appendix 2), built on what was once part of the Vickers shipyard and still overlooked by the huge building hall of the present BAE Systems ship and submarine building facility.

It is in here that some of the finest warship models ever built are displayed.

One example of this is the 1:48 Japanese battle cruiser Kongo designed by George Thurston. The model is now

5.2 The Agerholm is probably the most detailed model ever built. *(Photo by Naval Sea Systems Command)*

6.1 LST-542 class USS Chelan County. *(Photo by Naval Sea Systems Command)*

7.1 Another extraordinary model, the Austrian battleship Viribus Unitis. *(Photo Eduard Kompast)*

7.3 The workmanship and detail on this model is breathtaking to behold. *(Photo Eduard Kompast)*

7.2 Like the Agerholm the purpose of the Viribus Unitis is to show in great detail all the internal arrangements.*(Photo Eduard Kompast)*

8.1 (right) HMS Howe at 1:48 scale. *(Photo by kind permission of Glasgow Museum of Transport)*

8.2 Starboard side of HMS Howe.

gracing the entrance to the main display hall and carefully restored to its former glory by professional model makers EDM of Manchester UK.

For today's modeller it is a golden opportunity to view in detail the work of these master craftsmen of almost a century ago. The degree of detail is very evident in this close up of the amidships of Kongo **Photo 2.1**. As you look closely at the model you begin to appreciate how really good these modellers were. This is again illustrated in **Photo 2.2**.showing the after 14in turret. Note the deck fittings, which are either nickel-silver or copper.

Learning from the past - Photo Series 3

As mentioned this period was the nadir of British shipbuilding and by association the shipyard model. Remembering that the purpose was to impress so realism was not an issue, correctness was. Even though many of the fittings on the model were unpainted, they were fitted to give the clear impression that they would function and that is the acid test for any model builder. A good example of this is in this bed anchor arrangement on the pre-dreadnought battleship HMS Vengeance **Photo 3.1**.

Bed anchor

Here modellers can gain a real insight as to how a "Martins close stowing anchor" was secured to the anchor bed and the purpose of the "cathead davit" **Fig 3.1**. The study of models such as these has great benefits for the "amateur" modeller with an interest in warships of any period. Again a useful example is in the use of a "Bow Stopper" fitted to warships relying on the middle line capstan before the fitting of cable holders and was used to hold the cable as it was being hauled in, **Photo 3.2**.

Masts and rigging

More detail is revealed when examining masts and their rigging, not all of course are perfect replicas of the original but nonetheless give an insight into the period when the ship was built. **Photo 3.3** illustrates this point well showing the main mast of the pre-dreadnought battleship HMS Vengeance. Immediately below the control platform is the "shroud hoop" complete with eyes, shackle, thimble and shroud. The thimble is a circular or heart shaped ring, grooved to enable a rope to be spliced around it. The large single blocks made of brass form part of the topping lift and purchase for the main lifting derrick.

Ship's boats

Some of the most superb pieces of modelling can be seen in the ship's boat and again a wealth of information can be gleaned from how these boats were rigged to the methods by which they were stowed. Typical is the picture **Photo 3.4** of a cutter on the davits. Note the white "gripping band" diagonally securing the boat in place against what is called a gripping spar see **Fig 3. 2**.

Accommodation ladder and "Night Lifebuoy"

The accommodation ladder is faithfully reproduced on this fine model of the Japanese pre-dreadnought IJN Hatsuse of 1896 **Photo 3.5**, now an exhibit at Cragside House near Morpeth Northumberland UK; the one time home of the Armstrong Whitworth family. The drawing also gives some references to the materials used **Fig 3.4**. Once again these types of models reveal a wealth of information regarding the methods and practices of the time. Fittings such as the "night lifebuoy" can be seen very clearly in **Photo 3.6** fitted to a model of the armoured cruiser HMS Argyll at the Glasgow Museum of Transport. Interestingly, the light on the "night lifebuoy" is generated by calcium contained in metal cylinders at the sides of the framework, which is automatically activated by seawater and could burn for approximately 30 minutes.

9.1 Housed in the Musee de la Marine Paris are these 1:96 scale models of the battleship Richelieu and in the foreground the battle cruiser Dunkerque

10.1 Dave Abbot's award winning
"Ton" class minesweeper HMS
Iverston. *(Photo Dave Abbott)*

10.2 A superb 1:192 scale USS
Long Beach by Don Preul.

Presentation and finish - Photo Series 4

Not all models are presented in the most detailed way, and in keeping with less ornate models, hatches, doors even windows are drawn not made and fitted as separate items. This method is clearly demonstrated around parts of the bridge and deck housings on this model of a barbette battleship HMS Resolution of 1893 on display at Discovery Museum Newcastle upon Tyne, UK **Photo 4.1**. Not all models are to be found in museums and some can be traced to the most unusual of places.

Take for example this model of the armoured cruiser Rurik built in the model shop at Vickers of Barrow in 1908. Two were made, one for the company and the other for the client, which happened to be the Imperial Russian Navy. The Vickers model was discovered not in the museum but in the basement of Furness Hospital, in good condition and in a favourable environment, **Photo 4.2** (see colour section). It will be noted that the model is finished in grey but the bridge and fore and aft armoured conning positions are left as they were made in wood veneer, which was a standard practice of the time. Although the deck on the original was planked the deck on the model is painted in a buff finish to represent a Linoleum covering.

Many warship models were painted to match that of the original, this was particularly true of the years prior to WW2. Very few were actually painted in the camouflage schemes of the period and were represented in overall grey. The types of camouflage used will be discussed in more detail in Chapter 9.

The Agerholm model - Photo Series 5

The idea of a model cut away (either in part or from a full hull), to illustrate the internal layout is not new and goes back at least to the time of Navy Board models. But with the coming of steam, internal machinery, which included the power plant services, generators, turbines and latterly more complex power generation arrangements such as nuclear was shown. There was a need to see how all this would inter-relate within the confines of a hull. So the specialist section model was created. In effect this is more of an attempt to create the real ship in miniature but with the added advantage of being able to genuinely see how the many sections of the ship would work one to the other.

Without doubt the finest example of this technique is in the 1:24 scale model of the "Gearing" class destroyer USS Agerholm built by Gibbs and Cox, **Photo 5.1**. It is when you view the opposite side of the model that you really become mesmerised by the sheer volume of work, that to be fair is more model engineering than model ship building but to be impressed is not quite the right verb to describe this model. Every single piece of machinery as used on the full-size vessel was incorporated into the model, even down to the fresh water services, mess space ventilation and many other vital functions **Photo 5.2**.

LST 542 class USS Chelan County - Photo Series 6

This particular 1:48 model represents a sea-going, 2,100 ton LST and was designed to show the internal arrangements for loading and discharging payloads via a forward ramp with slopes of around 1 in 50. It will be noted that this type of LST is equipped with a smaller LCT6 riding "piggy back". This is visible amidships mounted atop of the main deck, **Photo 6.1**. When viewing the model from the opposite side it then becomes clear the reason for its construction. However the real skill of the model maker becomes apparent in Photo 6.2 where every piece of detail relating to the full-size LST is built into this extraordinary model.

"Atlanta" class - USS Juneau II

The standard of these builders' models (Gibbs & Cox) is something to behold even when built during wartime, as this 1:48 model of the Junuau II an "Atlanta" class cruiser built at Federal and completed in early February 1946, **Photo 6.3**.

Austrian Battleship Viribus Unitis - Photo Series 7

There are many examples in museums around the world of outstanding models that are on view to the general public. One such model is the Austrian dreadnought battleship Viribus Unitis taking pride of place at the Heersgeschichtliches

Museum of Military History in Vienna. Like the Agerholm model, the Viribus Unitis uses the same technique to show the exterior of the ship whilst having the interior completely exposed.

This 21,595 ton "Dreadnought" type battleship was laid down on the 24th May 1910 at the Stabilimento Tecnico Triestino shipyard and had the distinction of being the first battleship of any navy to be fitted with triple turrets. As first of a class of four ships consisting of SMS Tegetthoff, Prinz Eugen and Szent Istvan, Viribus Unitis was to become the fleet flagship. During the closing days of WW1, and as the Austro-Hungarian Empire was disintegrating, Viribus Unitis was inactive in Pola harbour, but was attacked and sunk on November 3rd 1918 by an Italian "Manatta", an early form of human torpedo.

Viribus Unitis - the model

The model was started after completion of the full-size ship but even though war intervened in August 1914, work on the model continued and was not completed until 1917. Photos show the incredible detail lavished on this model, first from a position on the portside looking aft **Photo 7.1** then the remarkable full hull view of the Viribus Unitis from the starboard side with a diagram explaining to the viewer the parts that make up the interior **Photo 7.2**.

The following photos illustrate how this type of presentation works for those viewing this model. Forward of the bridge is the armoured conning position with **Photo 7.3** giving a very clear impression of how the interior of the armoured tower was laid out including a run of voice pipes trunked up from decks below. Much more of this model deserves to be seen, sadly only a limited number of pictures can be included and do not do justice to this extraordinary model as only a visit to the Military Museum in Vienna will give the viewer a real appreciation of this magnificent warship model. Without overstating the fact, it could be said that the standard of workmanship is bordering on the artistic as these pictures of the turret, barbette and the magazine will testify, **Photo 7.4** (see colour section).

Glasgow Museum of Transport - Photo Series 8

The river Clyde was the home of many of the great shipyards and many of the great warships. Only a handful of shipyards now remain, yet the awe and prestige generated by Clyde built ships can still be appreciated in the Glasgow Museum of Transport, which ranks along with the Science Museum in London as one of the great Museums for the study of warship models. **Photos 8.1 – 8.2** illustrate this point well with the 1:48 model of the "King George V" class battleship HMS Howe.

Musee de la Marine Paris - Photo Series 9

For French warships probably one of the finest collections to browse and study is in the Musee de La Marine in Paris. Here are housed many of the warships from the period of sail through to the missile age. The collection of course includes the battleship Richelieu as featured in Chapter 1 and the battle cruiser Dunkerque, **Photo 9.1**.

The amateur warship model - Photo Series 10

The definition of the word amateur is a person who does something for love not money. Yet the word can also be used to define the level of skill. Yet many "amateur" models are made where the accuracy and quality of build can match many constructed professionally. It is also interesting to note that the division between working and static is becoming less well defined. Many working models have gained top awards at the highest levels of competition both in the United States and United Kingdom.

Many of the models shown in this chapter, which were built for and largely by the shipbuilding industry are often devoid of that touch of "realism" often appreciated as a hallmark of the "amateur". A number of scratch-built examples have been chosen not because they have been singled out as the best of their genre but because they represent what can be seen as the true qualities of the amateur model maker.

The first of these models was built by one of the UK's most accomplished ship modellers Dave Abbott, and is a fully working 1:48, scratch-built model of the "Ton" class minesweeper HMS Iveston, **Photos 10.1**. The hull was built up using plank-on-frame which, as a method of construction for model ships, will be discussed in detail in Chapter 5. His attention to detail and fidelity to the original, gained Dave Abbott a well-deserved Gold Medal at the 1995 Model Engineer Exhibition. Even such mundane items as the basket weave hull guards are included and are stored just abaft of the funnel. Our second example is a scratch-built static, 1:192 model of the Nuclear powered CGN USS Long Beach built by Don Preul, which illustrates well the unusual appearance of this revolutionary warship which was discussed at some length in Chapter 1, **Photo 10.2**.

Whilst discussing the quality of amateur built models there is also the aspect of uniqueness and originality in the choice of subject. This is clearly demonstrated by this model of the breastwork monitor HMS Cerberus built by Dave Abbott, **Photo 10-3** (see colour section). The amateur unlike the professional has the freedom of choice to build any type of warship model that appeals to his or her interest. There is of course no pressure on the amateur to fulfil a contract deadline that professional model maker or companies are under obligation to meet.

All of the models shown in this chapter both professional and amateur could not have been built without the basic ingredients of research. Even before commencing construction, there are a number of requirements that need to be taken into consideration, these and other helpful tips to preparation will be discussed in the following chapter.

Chapter Three

Research, plans and helpful publications

Knowing where to look and what to look for are in themselves as important as the modeller's ability to use various tools in the construction of a model. Research, which can be considered a catch all for acquiring information, whether it be plans, general notes or photos. And like the use of tools, research is a skill that needs to be mastered and improved upon. For example when seeking plans there is a basic formula as to what constitutes an essential to build a model and what does not. Equally having the knowledge to know what to ask for when approaching a resource centre such as a museum or University, saves time, money and the possibility of being disappointed.

Research

As mentioned in the closing paragraph of Chapter 2, research is one of the most important aspects of building any model ship as it is intertwined with just about every part of the build. The amount of research required can be dependent on the type of vessel being built and to a large extent whether the model is built from scratch or is part of a semi kit or full kit. Most of the latter two come with ready-made parts and therefore much of the "research" has already has been incorporated. Nonetheless, some level of refinement could still be applied to enhance and improve on what a semi kit or kit provides.

Research for scratch building can be much more involved as nearly every aspect of such a build needs to be carefully

Fig 1 General Arrangement general arrangement drawing *(Drawing Jacobin Plans)*

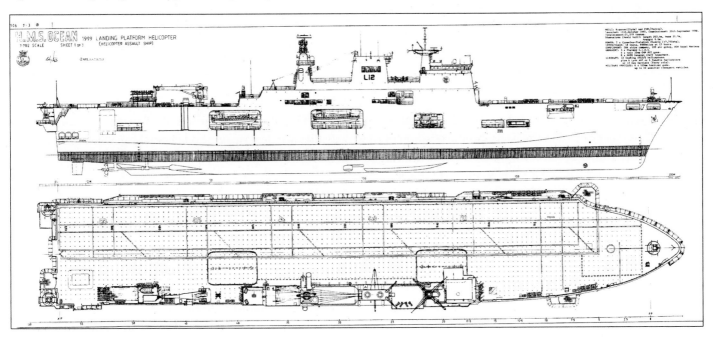

Fig 3 right Body plan drawing which gives the shape of the hull sections at a given position along the hull.

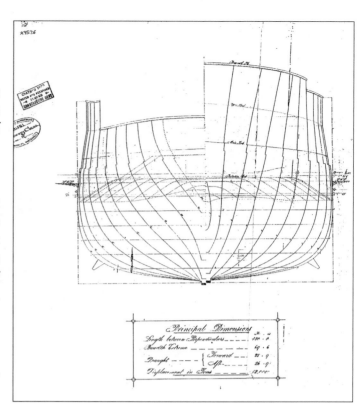

prepared, from acquiring a suitable drawing to searching out any relevant documentation relating to the construction of the ship and the procuring, where possible, a good set of quality and relevant (period of build) photographs.

Where to start

First and foremost is the choice of subject. Assuming that the approach is scratch building then it is most desirable to consider what is available with regard to information first and foremost of which is a reasonable set of drawings. The choice for the modeller is then to select the most relevant of the drawings available. At the very minimum these should consist of:

1 GA - General Arrangements drawing

A drawing, which will illustrate the outer shape of the hull including position of superstructure and fittings **Fig 1.2**

Fig 2 Sheer plan/line drawing. *(Drawing Jacobin Plans)*

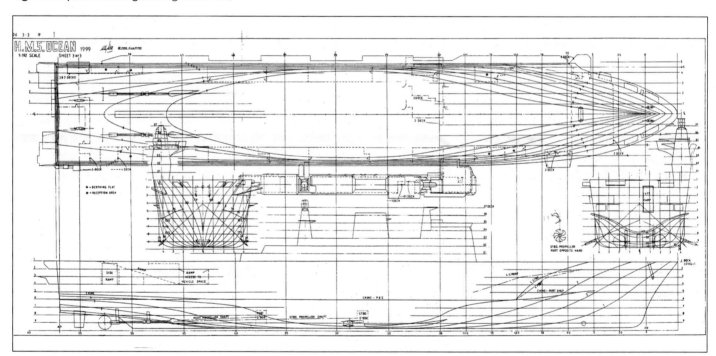

2 Sheer plan

A side view of the hull, which gives the general outline of the ship. The sheer or rise in the deck and the position of the load waterline. The accepted convention is for the drawing to show the ship with the bow pointing to the right **Fig 2**.

3 Body plan

This will provide the modeller with the shape of the moulded sections at given points along the hull that will correspond to the vertical lines shown on the sheer plan. The forward sections of the ship are shown on the right side of the body plan whilst the after section is drawn on the left-hand side **Fig 3**.

4 Rig

This will show the positions of any stay wires, ratlines, halyards, wireless rigging and general rig, which may include dressing lines and shrouds.

5 Half Breadth

This type of drawing is not always included but gives the shape of the decks and the waterline which are formed by the intersection of the surface of the ship with the horizontal planes as shown in **Fig 2**.

6 Shell expansion drawings

Not always necessary but essential if the outer shell plating

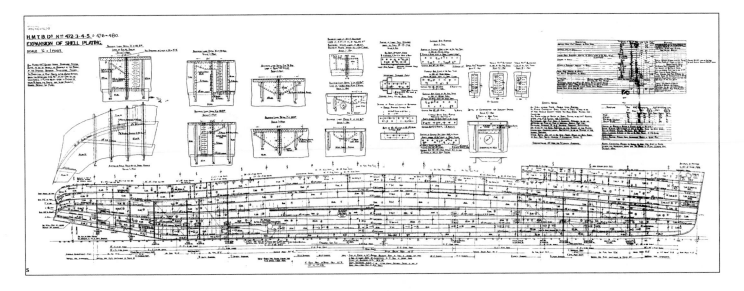

Fig 4 Shell expansion drawing outlines the actual shape of the plating on to a flat surface. *(Drawing University of Glasgow Archive)*

is to be shown. This type of drawing has been expanded transversely illustrating the "actual" shape of the plating on to a flat sheet of paper as if direct from the hull hence the very unusual shape, **Fig 4**.

Photo 1 Half-block plating model of HMS Achilles.

The half block model

This half block model of the "Leander" class light cruiser HMS Achilles was also used to show the exact positioning of the plates which would have been used as a reference when building the full-size vessel and can provide the same information for model builders, **Photo 1**.

Resource centres such as museums and libraries require, where possible, for modellers to be specific i.e. state requirements such as GA, lines, rig etc. However the next step is to locate where a set of drawings are most likely to be stored for a specific warship. First locate the name of the builder. As a general reference it is very useful to access books such as

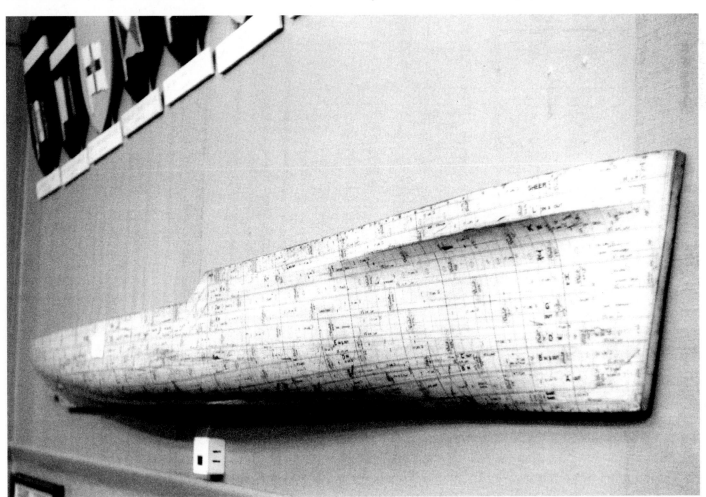

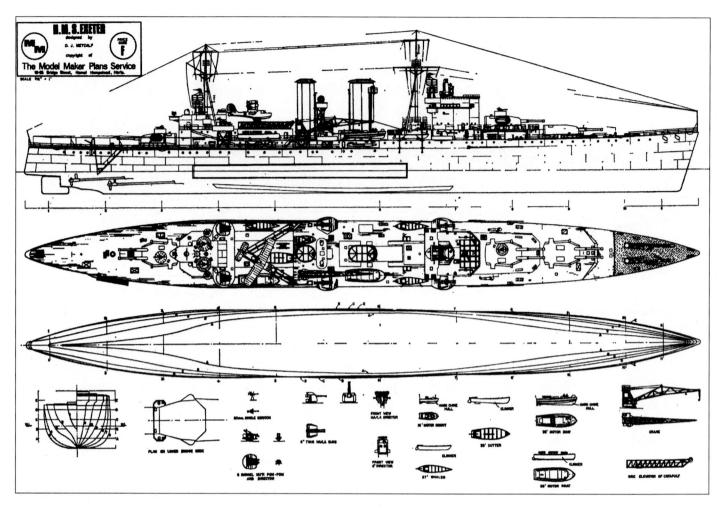

Fig 5 Basic model makers drawing of HMS Exeter *(Model Boats Plans Service)*

Fig 6 Comprehensive model maker's superstructure and fittings drawing
(Drawing Jacobin Plans)

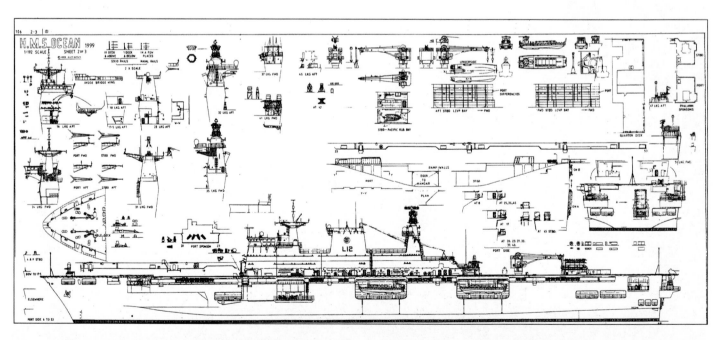

"Warships of World War 2" by Collage and Lenton or "US Warships of World War 2" by Paul H Silverstone. These will list the date of launch and completion but more importantly for the modelmaker, the shipyard and its location. Generally speaking most preserved drawings from English shipyards are now kept at the National Maritime Museum in Greenwich, although some are still retained by their local maritime or city museum. However, archive material associated with Scottish shipyards particularly those on the Clyde, are housed either at the University of Glasgow or at the Mitchell Library in

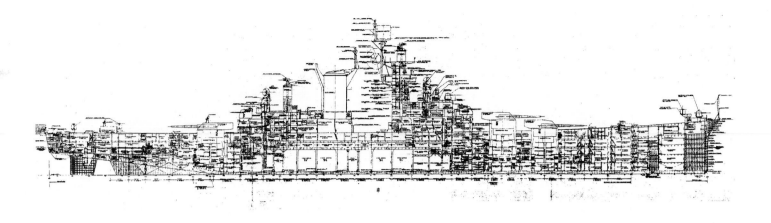

Fig 7 Inboard profile drawing of the "large cruiser" CB-1 USS Alaska extracted from the "General Book of Plans". *(National Archive)*

Glasgow, A list of present addresses for resource centres are listed in Appendix 2.

Appendix 2 also lists the name and contact information for unofficial sources such as "Floating Dry Dock" in the USA and John Lambert in the UK.

Photo 2 Bridge and island superstructure on the LPH HMS Ocean.

Bow lines and buttock lines

Also found on the Sheer plan are what are termed bow and buttock lines these must "fair up" or be consistent with the half breadth and body plans. The bow and buttock lines must cross the level lines in the sheer plan at points squared up from the corresponding intersections in the half breadth, and also must intersect with stations at points which are squared across from the corresponding intersections in the body plan.

Types of drawings

Most drawings that are available, whether those drawn by the shipyard or by the model maker should possess the very minimum amount of information that the modeller will require. However the quality and amount of constructional

Photo 3 A highly detailed picture of a Visual Gun Director aboard the Type 12 Frigate HMS Plymouth. *(Museum ship)*

information can vary from a simple GA and body plan as illustrated in this 1:200 scale drawing of the cruiser HMS Exeter provided by the "MM" plans service **Fig 5**, to a more comprehensive set of drawings which include the detailing of fittings, even isometric sketches, often drawn to a larger scale and illustrated specifically for the model maker. An example of this approach is shown in **Fig 6** of the LPH HMS Ocean, a set of comprehensive modellers' drawings prepared by Jacobin in the UK. See Appendix 1. Here the bridge and mainmast are clearly illustrated as separate drawings and shown in various elevations. This equally comprehensive treatment is also given to fittings such as the crane and LCVPs.

General Book of Plans - official plans source for USN warships

Builders drawings can in fact provide less information particularly regarding fittings, like ships boats etc. which are often presented as an outline and show little or no detail that the modeller would find useful. It is here that further research becomes necessary. In **Fig 7** the builders drawing of the "Large cruiser" USS Alaska is shown. Taken from the "General Book of Plans", an official source of GA drawings,

although omitting lines and body plan. Unlike the modeller's draught, the internal parts of the ship are clearly seen and through sections are also provided, which illustrate the deck spaces at given points along the hull.

Photographs

Whether building from scratch, from kit or semi-scratch, photos are one of the most useful methods of accurately identifying various parts of the drawing such as fittings and their location and position in relationship to other fittings. Although in this instance photos of the builder's model are being used. Equally any part of the ship that can be clearly identified can be used in conjunction with the drawing. A good example of this in practice is in the use of the Jacobin drawing of HMS Ocean, which is a particularly well-detailed example and can be clearly identifiable with the photos of the full-size ship. As such, any current modifications can be identified and incorporated into the model. This detailed photograph of the bridge and superstructure **Photo 2** graphically illustrate how useful photo identification can be for the modeller.

The problem with many simpler representative modellers' drawings like those of the Exeter is that they are just that "representative", therefore photographs can be of only marginal benefit. Although the model produced can look reasonably good, the consensus of opinion is that model

apply if the measurements are known. This is where choice of scale now becomes clear in relationship to transport and storage. A graphic example of this can be drawn from **Photos 11.2 & 11.3** In **Photo 11.2** a model is shown of the German aircraft carrier Graf Zeppelin by Canadian modeller Joseph Kovacs built to a scale of 1:144. Using the formula given then this model will measure a very manageable 71.83 x 9.83in. Contrast this with **Photo 11.3** showing a 1:50 Graf Zeppelin built by German modeller Rolf Streubel. This very large model measures 5.26 x 0.64m and weighs 260kgs.

A further example of scale versus size can be gained in this 1:72 scratch-built model of a Soviet "Sovremennyy" class DDG. The prototype is 511ft in length x 57ft in beam, resulting in a model 85in long x 9.5in beam **Photo 11.4** (see colour section).

This formula can be applied to any model ship and at a glance will help the modeller decide on a choice of scale to suit circumstances. When all is said and done, there is little point or satisfaction gained if the model is so large as to make transport and storage impossible. Equally, a model can be made of a large warship that is so small as to make sailing such a model a hazardous exercise. There is a level of compromise that will need to be made in order that the subject and scale are the right choice.

11.2 Although at a modest 1:144 scale for working models this Graff Zeppelin comes out at a reasonable 71.83inches. *(Photo Joseph Kovacs)*

Types and methods of construction - Photo Series 12

Kits are probably the most popular form of construction for building model warships, where almost all of the necessary items to complete a successful model are provided in a box. An example of this is the Deans Marine kit of a "Narvik" class German destroyer, **Photo 12.1**.

11.3 Much larger models are truly impressive but have a major problem when it comes to transport. *(Author's collection)*

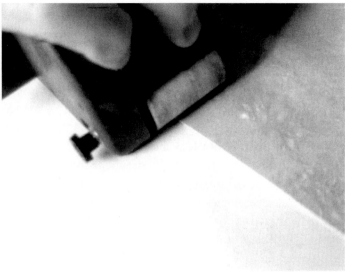

12.3 Scratch building takes time but is immensely rewarding.

13.1 Preparing the inside of a GRP hull.

The second option is a semi-scratch/semi-kit built warship model where the hull is GRP or styrene of commercial origin and many of the fittings can also be purchased from just a small percentage to a full 100% as in this Fleetscale HMS Tyne, **Photo 12.2**.

The third type of construction scratch building, is where the modeller makes the hull (regardless of method of build), superstructure, and a high percentage of the fittings. An example can be seen in **Photo 12.3** of the Soviet Aviation Cruiser Moskva.

The above can be seen as a clarification of the possible options available. Later in this chapter is an explanation of the work needed to prepare types of warship models for the later stages of the build. For scratch building this will include

the advised sequences of construction, and the preparation needed to successfully install such items as running gear/shafts/A frames/rudders/and radio control equipment the installation of which will be dealt with in the following chapter.

Human nature being what it is, this definition of construction type can become blurred as the challenge of building from scratch, a model that is not available in any other form, can override the level of ability. Equally anyone can "learn on the job" but as with so many skills, it is often better to start at a lower level and learn the skills progressively.

Warship models available in kit form, particularly from well-established manufactures, provide a comprehensive

13.2 The use of electrical tape reduces the possibility of damage when drilling into GRP.

13.3 Gently filing out the anchor hawse opening.

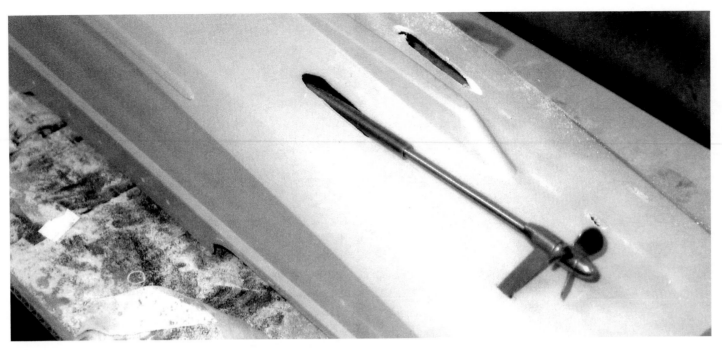

13.4 The openings in a GRP hull are enlarged to accept propeller shaft and "A" frame.

methodology of construction as part of their instructions usually accompanied by a plan and reference drawings. These show how sections are built up but more importantly, how they relate to other parts of the kit. This has a direct benefit in helping the builder understand the building cycle.

Much of the methodology is already thought through plus the bonus of a cross over onto semi-scratch building. As if to underline the real value of starting with a kit, this initial approach actually introduces the would-be model warship builder to the methodology necessary when building using other types of construction.

Starting with any GRP hull the first step is to check for signs of twisting. This fault is not uncommon in a freshly moulded hull and there are remedies that can be used to re-align it.

With a relatively thin hull, immersion in hot water or subjecting it to overall heat causes the GRP to become very malleable allowing the hull to be manipulated back to its proper form. More drastic measures may involve fitting an internal frame but generally some manipulation will be sufficient.

Preparation of GRP Hulls - Photo Series 13

Preparation work on a GRP hull will be the same whether the hull forms part of a kit or is used as part of a semi-scratch model. This will involve a number of stages:

1. Smoothing down the internal upper edge of the hull to take the gunwale stringer.

Tools required are either a sanding block with medium/coarse paper or a power sander as in **Photo 13.1**. This makes easy work of smoothing the inside upper edge.

2. Drilling and cutting out. This may include cutting openings into the hull for the anchor hawse pipes, wash ports or openings in the bulwarks, condenser ports and portholes if any. Tools required include a small drill (with variable speed if possible), a selection of bits. When drilling into GRP it's helpful to place a small strip of electrical tape over the area to be drilled, this will avoid the problem of the bit slipping or shattering any of the surrounding gel coat. An example of this is shown on a 1:96 GRP hull of HMS Pegasus of the hawse opening for the anchor, **Photo 13.2**. The use of a small round coarse file to enlarge the hawse opening on a 1:96 OPV HMS Mersey is shown in **Photo 13.3**.

3. Preparation for fitting the running gear comprising propeller shaft(s) and rudder posts. Generally there will be dimples or raised spots on the under surface of the hull indicating the exact position. Large openings for a propeller tube may well require a series of connecting holes to be drilled around the area where the tube enters the hull that can be connected by use of a file. Once an opening of sufficient size has been made, a file can be used to expand and progressively lengthen the opening to allow the outer propeller tube to take up the correct angle to correspond with the plan, **Photo 13.4**.

"A" Frames

The preparation follows the sequence described above. A series of holes is drilled in the position where the "A" frame will enter the hull. As with the other openings, a small flat file will be sufficient to form the correct size and shape of the opening. The "A" frame as in **Photo 13.4** can be seen in place supporting the end of the shaft.

Making the rudder - Photo Series 14

Making up a rudder is quite a straightforward job either in metal, wood or plastic:

1. Select the rudderpost and cut to size. This can be made of

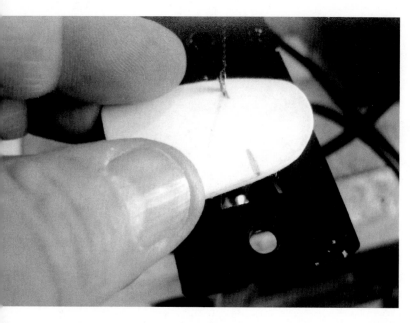

14.1 Making provision on the rudder profile for the rudderpost.

14.2 Checking the shape and position.

brass rod or stainless steel.

2. Cut out a profile shape of the rudder as per the drawing and make a cut into the profile where the rudderpost is seated, **Photo 14.1**.

3. Open up the cut to the same diameter of the post. The post is then inserted into the rudder, **Photo 14.2**.

4. Laminations are glued to either side of the flat core shape of the rudder to give the required section, **Photo 14.3**.

5. A small amount of filler such as Isopon P38 is mixed and spread using a plastic squeegee, **Photo 14.4**.

6. When the filler is firmly set, (usually in about 10 minutes

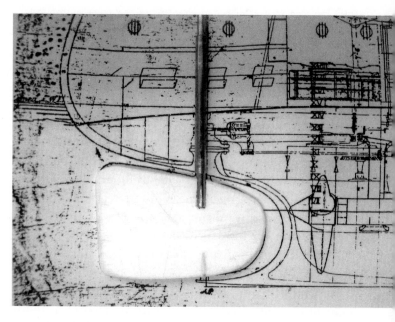

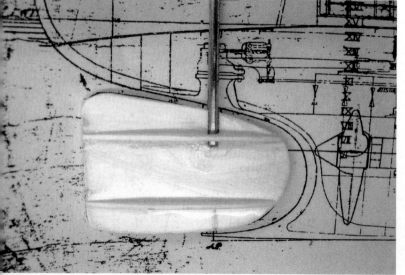

14.3 Inserting the profile formers.

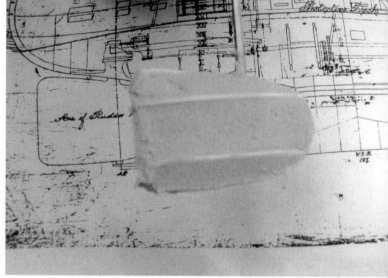

14.4 Using fillers to build up the shape between the profiles.

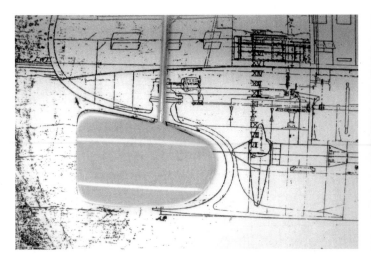

14.5 The rudder is sanded down to give a smooth, curved profile

15.1 Provision is made along the edge of the hull so the deck is seated flush with the top edge.

depending on the amount of activator) the rudder can be sanded down using "wet or dry" abrasive until the surface is smooth **Photo 14.5**. The rudder is now ready to be fitted into place along with the propeller shaft. See Chapter 6.

Fitting the gunnel stringer to a GRP hull - Photo Series 15

Once the openings in the GRP hull have been made, the upper gunnel stringer can be fitted into place. The purpose of this is to give support to the deck around the edge plus a support for the bearers. They will also provide additional strength to the edge of the hull. A range of clamps will be required to keep the stringers in place while the adhesive is

16.1 A totally scratch-built Soviet battle cruiser Kirov.

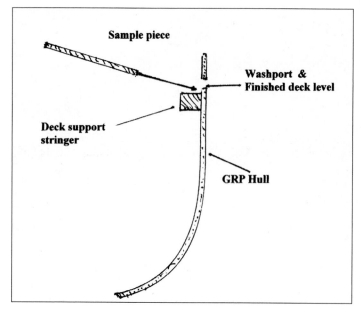

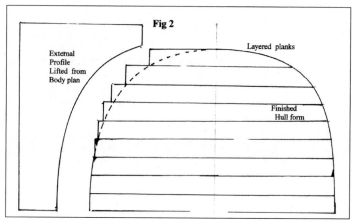

Fig 16.1 External profile (template) used for bread and butter construction.

Fig 15.1 Checking the correct deck seating depth against the inside of the hull.

16.2 A bread and butter hull formed using external profiles.

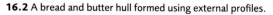

setting.

First cut the upper stringer to length. They can be made from plastic strip or 4mm square ramin. Cut a sample piece of the deck to length, which can be used to check the correct seating depth in relation to any openings, wash ports and the finished main deck level, **Fig 5.1**. It is advisable wherever possible that the main deck should always seat inside the hull not on to the top edge as this latter type of joint is weak and is more likely to crack open at a later date, **Photos 15.1**. Further preparation of GRP hulls will be discussed in Chapters 6-7.

Methods of scratch building a hull - Photo Series 16

Building a model from scratch could be considered the ultimate achievement in model building and can be immensely rewarding. One of the clear advantages is that unlike building from a kit or a commercial GRP hull, there is a wider range of subjects to choose from, as the only limitation is information generally relating to drawings and photographs.

Within the term scratch-building there are various methods that can be used to achieve the same results. A model can be made from timber, metal, plastic or any combination of all three materials. The techniques employed can vary from wooden plank on frame, double diagonal planked construction, "bread and butter" lamination through to all-metal.

The one single advantage when scratch-building is that the builder is not reliant on hull or kit availability but far more on information sources as well as personal skill.

Photo 16.1 illustrates this point well and shows an all scratch-built model of the Soviet battle cruiser Kirov built by Soviet era enthusiast Colin McDonald from plans drawn up by himself using a limited number of pictures. However this is the exception not the rule.

Assuming that the builder has acquired a set of suitable drawings either from a commercial source as mentioned in Chapter 3 or available through one of a number of museum archive services, construction methods can be chosen. The

17.1 Forming the keel with 4mm marine ply. Note the hull frames are cut and ready to be fitted.

17.3 For accuracy hull planking is commenced from the centre line of the keel working outwards, first on one side then the other.

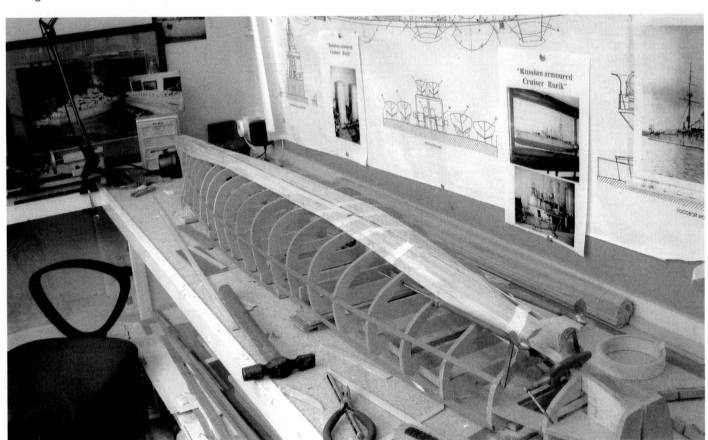

17.2 Each frame is accurately squared up.

method can in some respects be dependent on whether the model is to be working or static. As this book deals mainly with working models then methods such as "bread and butter" construction (particularly for larger working models) may well be impractical but remain useful for smaller scales.

"Bread and butter" construction

Each shape shown on the half breadth plan is copied onto timber planks equal in thickness to the lines shown on the side profile. If the model is to be working then a portion of the inside is removed. Once all the layers are cut to size, they are bonded together. At this point the shape of the hull takes on a step like appearance. To achieve the correct hull form "external profiles" (templates) are used which are lifted

from the body plan (see Chapter3), **Fig 16.1**. Each profile corresponds to a section along the hull and using these as guides, the hull is power sanded or planed down with the profiles being continually checked against the hull until the true shape is formed. Because of its strength this method is also favoured for making the "plug" or pattern from which a mould is made for casting GRP hulls, **Photo 16.2**.

Building a hull using plank-on-frame construction - Photo Series 17

Once a suitable drawing is to hand, first task is to lift the sections from the body plan. This is a process whereby each half section or frame is copied either by tracing (see below) or photocopying which is then pasted onto card. There may be any number of hull sections shown from 1 through to 35 or more, each conforming to the shape of the hull at a given point along the profile drawing. Remember that when transferring this for reproduction, say on timber, there is only half the shape. It's worth remembering that the body plan shows the full beam of the ship, thus when transferring the shapes the thickness of the hull planking needs to be taken into account and the sections reduced accordingly in order to maintain the measurements shown on the body plan for the finished hull.

Each frame is cut to size from 4mm marine ply using either the band saw or Vibro saw. The band saw is preferable for initial cutting out of the frames whilst the Vibro saw is best suited to removing the internal part of the frame.

Note that there are a series of cutouts made into the frame.

17.4 To add strength, splay any joints in the planking and, where possible, avoid butt jointing.

PHOTO 2 Right: A Modern construction hall. *(Photo by kind permission of VT)*

PHOTO 4 Below: CVN-75 Harry S Truman *(Official US Navy photo)*

PHOTO 8 above: Replenishment at sea. RFA Fort Victoria and the CV HMS Invincible. *(Photo Crown Copyright)*

PHOTO 23 right: A 1:96 model of the Sverdlov.

Left: October 2006, roll-out for HMS Clyde a River class OPV (H). This, the first ship to be built entirely in Portsmouth naval base for nearly 40 years.

PHOTO 31 overleaf left: "Ticonderoga" class USS Chosin CG-65 *(US Navy photo)*

PHOTO 30 overleaf right: CGN-38 USS Virginia July 1985 *(Photo Nobie Smith)*.

PHOTO 35 above: First of the class DDG-51 USS Arleigh Burke June 1991 *(Photo Nobe Smith)*

PHOTO 37 below: Gracefull lines of the stretched Type 42 DDG HMS Manchester.

PHOTO 44 right: HMS Ocean LPH Landing Platform Helicopter *(Crown Copyright)*

PHOTO 48 left: One of the builder's models of the CSS Alabama housed at The Williamson Art Gallery Birkenhead.
(Photo by kind permission of Wirral Archive Service)

PHOTO 10.3 Right: Dave Abbot's very unusual model of the breastwork monitor HMS Cerberus. *(Photo Dave Abbott).*

Opposite below: The author's workshop.

PHOT 4.2 right: The Vickers built Russian armoured cruiser Rurik.
(By kind permission of Barrow in Furness Hospital)

PHOTO 7.4 right: Every item of engineering is included especially so in the barbette and turrets.*(Photo Eduard Kompast)*

PHOTO 11.1 left: A 1:128 scale HMS Hood built up on a GRP (Glass Reinforced Plastic) hull.

PHOTO 29.2 opposite top: The completed armoured tower on Blucher.

PHOTO 30.4 opposite below left: The completed superstructure, which lifts clear of slightly sloping sides.

PHOTO 30.5 opposite below right: This superstructure required a dedicated case to protect the delicate radar arrays.

PHOTO 11.4 below: A 1:72 this Sovremennyy offers larger scale with a manageable model.

PHOTO 48.1 above: Ted Parr's authentically presented CVN 68 USS Nimitz with its well-researched air group.

PHOTO 53.6 left: Typical fire fighting hose stowage aboard ships of the USN.

PHOTO 63.1 above: Western approaches camouflage scheme

PHOTO 64.2 below: Accurately camouflaged CL49 USS St Louis by Don Preul.

PHOTO 65.2 left: CV-18 USS Wasp 1971, decommissioned in 1972. Weathering takes its toll. *(Photo Nobie Smith)*

PHOTO 69.1 right: An evocative HMS Kent in Victorian Livery.

PHOTO 66.1 below: Superbly applied weathering technicque to a Belgium flower class corvette Godetia.

PHOTO 72.3 above: Blucher in good trim condition.

PHOTO 81.2 right: Russian circular coastal defence ship using no less than 6 shafts.

17.5 planking of the hull is almost complete.

The notches on the top of the frame are for the longitudinal members whilst those around the top and lower edges are for gunnel and bracing stringers, the purpose of which will become clearer as we progress. It will also be noted that the cutouts in each frame for the keel should correspond with the width and depth and be a firm push fit on to the keel.

17.6 Once the hull is planked and sanded a small amount of filler can be applied.

Laying the keel and setting the frames

With the frames cut to size, the keel can be made using 4mm marine ply. As with the frames, the shape, length and depth is marked out on the main profile drawing.

The length, which takes into account the stem and stern post, is made up of two sections and for this example (the Russian armoured cruiser Rurik) has a depth of 25mm and spliced in the mid-section using a scarf joint. The centre third is doubled in width to give additional strength around the joint and using "Extramite" or equivalent resin wood glue, each of the pieces that make up the keel are bonded together, **Photo 17.1.**

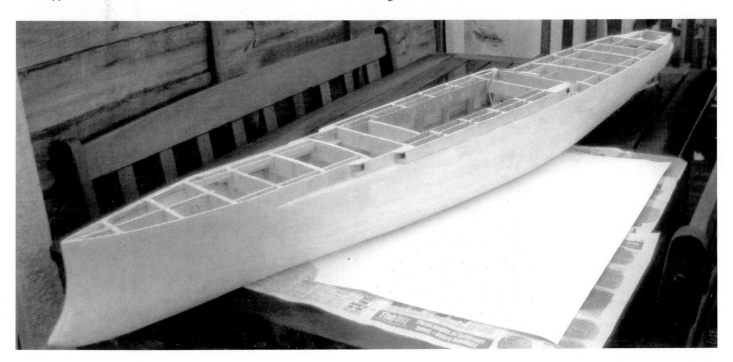

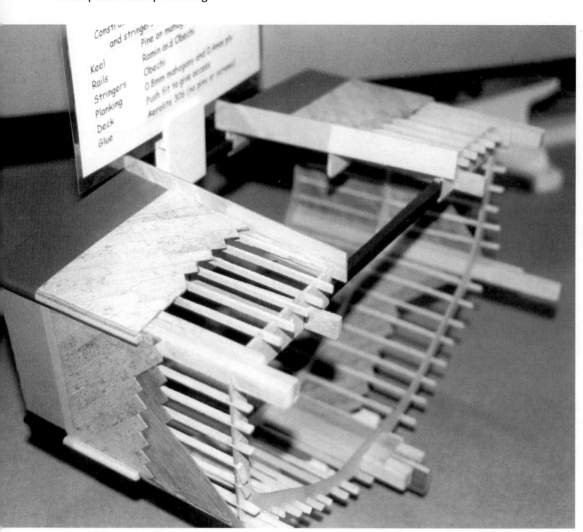

18.1 A hull construction demonstrator showing the methodology in double diagonal planking.

19.1 An all brass working LCVP landing craft. *(Photo H Barrow)*

To assist in maintaining good alignment, all of the frames should retain the centre lines used during the transfer of the sections from the body plan. The idea being that when all the frames are being set into place, the centre lines can be used to visually line them up fore and aft, helping to check and maintain the overall symmetry of the hull.

The cut outs for stringers and longitudinal bearers are also checked out for alignment. The positions of these bearers can be determined by the eventual location of any part of the deck or superstructure that will need to be removed for access. Also at this stage keel supports are set into place either side of the keel fore and aft and in the centre. These can take the form of lengths of timber approximately 50mm long x 25mm square.

Setting the frames

With the keel fixed firmly to the building board, each frame can be permanently set in place in conjunction with the upper bearers and stringers. Alignment both fore and aft and vertically must be constantly checked with the aid of a setsquare, **Photo 17.2**.

Once all the frames are in place and the adhesive has hardened the entire skeletal form can be lifted clear of the keel support clamps.

Planking the hull

Although still in its basic form the shape is beginning to resemble a hull and can be prepared for planking. The hull is inverted keel-up and fixed to the building board using a similar method to that used for clamping the keel. The stem and stern posts are secured to the building board taking account of any "shear and counter shear" with packing pieces being inserted under frames where necessary. Small lengths of timber are also secured either side of three or four frames "athwartships", (depending on the length of the model), to secure the hull firmly in place whilst planking.

Any type of easily manipulated timber from balsa to ply can be used successfully to plank a hull. However from experience, lime is both malleable and easy to work. The objective is to minimise the effort and the work required to achieve a good surface with the very minimum of filling, once the planking is completed.

First steps to planking a hull

Commencing from the centre of the keel or just off centre, the first plank is laid followed by the second to port then to starboard. This helps maintain continuity of form minimising the possibility of distortion. Each plank is firmly bonded to the previous plank and held in place with small brass pins and masking tape until the adhesive is set, **Photo 17.3**. As the curve of the bilge is reached the edges should be chamfered to present a good surface to each joint. Equally butt joints between each plank fore and aft should be avoided and a scarfed joint used wherever possible, **Photo 17.4**. Note that adhesive is applied to the entire length of the plank.

It will be seen that a number of planks around the bilge are also "feathered" and chamfered on both edges to present a longer splay in order that the joints are maintained. Here the planking is almost complete save for the top edge, **Photo 17.5**.

The top edge plank or gunnel may also need to be feathered to follow the sheer line, which in Rurik rises both fore and aft.

Once almost covered, the hull can be released from the building board and turned over and the remaining planks to the gunnel can be fitted. At this stage any blocking out to the stem or stern can be carried out. Obeche is a good timber to use for this having both a fine grain and being easy to work. Reflecting the period 1905, Rurik had recesses built into the hull along the deck edge fore and aft for the secondary armament, generally referred to as waist level guns.

Fitting the deck and rubbing down

When the hull planking is complete, the deck is cut to size. Bear in mind that the deck will be seated within the hull and therefore will be cut slightly smaller than indicated by the plan. When fitted, the deck should be flush with the top of the gunwale planking. The rationale is to increase the strength along the deck edge whilst minimising the problem of stress cracks occurring were the deck edge joins the hull.

As the planks are of lime wood, sanding down is a less arduous job than with some timbers however suitable care should be taken. Always wear a dust mask and eye protectors. From experience I prefer to sand by hand using a sanding pad and selected grades of paper. Progressively sanding the hull with each grade until the surface joints are merged with the overall shape and a smooth surface is produced. . With this operation completed the next stage is to seal the surface with a mix of turpentine substitute and clear varnish.

The surface can be gently "dusted" with an aerosol of matt black when dry to touch. This has the effect of highlighting the hollows (small particles) and humps (larger particles), making it easier to identify the exact areas where fillers need be applied.

Applying Fillers to the hull

Fillers can be any one of a number of proprietary brands for example P38 or Bondoglass. Target only those areas, which need to be filled as blanket covering just makes unnecessary work. The better the hull is planked and sanded, the less filler will be needed.

Once set the filler can be gently rubbed down with a medium fine "wet and dry" abrasive not forgetting to apply a little common sense regarding health and safety, by following the basic rule of rubbing down in a well-ventilated area and always wearing some form of protective mask.

Rubbing down and adding filler may need to be repeated depending on how well the hull has been prepared. A covering of primer will help in identifying any further parts of the

19.2 Litho plate used for building superstructures and fittings.

hull that will require filling. A point will be reached when the surface of the hull will be completely uniform, **Photo 17.6**. The paint used as a primer goes under the name of "Hi-build" and is acrylic based and will fill any minor scratches or imperfections that remain on the surface of the hull. The hull can now remain unpainted until further constructional work is undertaken. Incidentally any openings in the hull such as portholes and hawse pipes for the anchor can be made at any time after treatment with fillers. It helps to keep the hull rigid with bolts through a portable baseboard into the keel during the remainder of the build. The holes made can be easily filled when the hull is ready for any final touching up.

Preparation for painting and painting plank on frame hulls will be discussed in detail in Chapter 9.

Double diagonal planking - Photo Series 18

Double diagonal planking is applied in two distinct layers at 40 to 45 degrees to one another and unlike the plank on frame method discussed above, the frames have a greater number of stringers, usually closely spaced. An example of this method can be seen in this demonstrator constructed by Roy Skeets for his award winning MGB, **Photo 18.1**. His model follows the original builder's method whereby the

stringers would have been extended to the deck. It will be noted that the first layer is fitted at approximately 45 degrees aft whilst the second layer is at 45 degrees forward. This method allows each layer to be of a thickness where each individual layer would be relatively weak but with two layers of 0.4mm ply would be many times the strength of a single 0.8mm layer of the same material.

Metal construction - Photo Series 19

Although outside the scope of this book, it is worth mentioning metal as a method of construction for scratch-built models. An all brass LCVP built by Harry Barrow to a scale of 1:24 is shown in Photo 19.1. Models to this exacting standard are often constructed as model engineering projects and as such are not working models. However this is a fully functioning model and follows the original prototype in every minute detail even down to the rivets securing the deck house plating. A further use for metal is in this 1:96 scale "Ford" class seaward defence ASW boat by Allan Whitham. The hull is of double diagonal planked construction (see Chapter 4), but all the superstructure including all the fittings are made from litho plate, a material that has the properties of metal but can be worked like styrene, **Photo 19.2**.

Chapter Six

Internal fitting-out

Internal fitting-out - Photo Series 20

The layout of the installation of such equipment as shafts, rudders, linkages, servos and batteries is conditional on space available regardless of the type of hull construction. Although the open area within a GRP hull offers greater access than say a scratch built plank on frame hull of equivalent size, providing the builder with much greater freedom to achieve the ideal layout. **Photo 20.1** demonstrates how the removable superstructure for a 1:96 model of BB55 USS North Carolina has been arranged to provide equipment access. Compare this to a scratch built 1:125 plank on frame hull of the aviation carrier Moskva **Photo 20.2**. Regardless of construction, it is good practice for any internal hardware to be fitted prior to the fitting of the deck. Although to some extent positioning of the hardware is conditional on the location of the superstructure, any limitations imposed on access by deck housings needs to be carefully thought through.

Providing entry into the hull need not be totally reliant on the superstructure. The entire main deck to any natural break can be made removable. Whilst this method does indeed provide greater freedom of access, the problem of providing good water integrity can be brought into question. From personal choice and experience it is often better not to remove the entire deck but confine access to a limited area. This is demonstrated in practice with the removal of only part of the flight deck on a 1:144 Nimitz, **Photo 20.3** and as seen in Chapter 1.

Thus the locations of any internal fitments such as motors,

20.1 The area of access provided into the hull of a 1:96 scale North Carolina.

receiver, rudder servo, speed controller and batteries will now be determined by that access.

Take for example the rudder servo. Logic would state that the shortest link between the rudder tiller and the servo arm would be best because there would be no undue strain on the servomotor or flex in the pushrod. Therefore the servo would either have to be permanently concealed beneath the deck or provision made for additional access. As a servo is an electro-mechanical device if it's going to go wrong then it will if it is in the most awkward part of the hull to access.

Warship models by their very design are not altogether conducive to the easy siting of such fittings as rudder servos etc. Once again, serious thought has to be given to the exact location of each of the components that make up the internal hardware so as to avoid the very problems outlined above (in kit models this process is generally provided for). For semi-scratch or scratch-built models, planning for this needs to be undertaken before the running gear is fitted. First work out from the drawing, the area of the superstructure that is likely to be detachable from the deck. Assuming that the sizes of the hardware elements are known, (motor size, battery size and capacity, size of speed controller) work out the relative positions of the rudder servo, motors /couplings. Now choose a site for the battery box that should be located so that the battery can be lifted through the deck opening provided. The speed controller should be located where it

20.2 Although there are sufficient space the bulkheads on this 1:125 scale Moskva caused some initial problems.

20.3 With carriers and their expanse of flight deck access is a compromise.

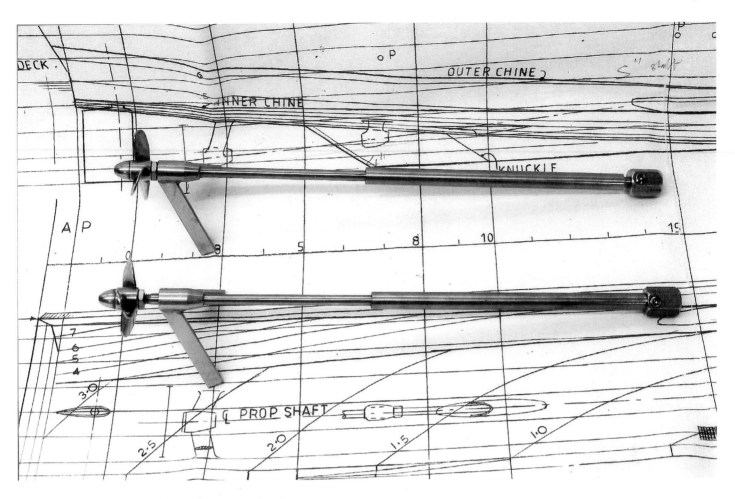

21.1 Bespoke made running gear for a 1:96 OPV HMS Mersey

21.2 "A" frame and shaft as fitted to the FFG Donald B Beary.

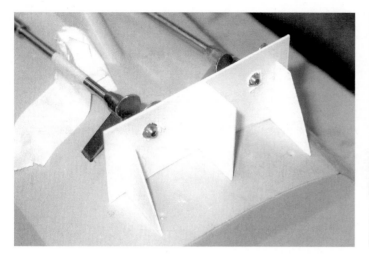

21.3 A simple but effective jig applied to maintain shaft alignment accuracy.

22.1 Whilst securing the rudderpost to the hull a jig such as this maintains the rudder in the correct position.

22.2 The servo arm is sited well forward for easy adjustment. Note that the linkage from servo to rudder arm is through a plastic sleeve.

can be removed should the need arise.

As an example, a series of photos has been produced that illustrate how this train of thought develops commencing with the installation of the shaft, "A" frame and rudder posts on a 1:96 GRP hull of HMS Mersey.

Installing the drive train - Photo Series 21

A GRP hull had been chosen to best illustrate the method of installing the drive train, although the principles apply to any hull. Propeller tubes and shaft can be either fabricated or purchased complete from a number of bespoke manufacturers that make to order. Providing there are drawings available then running gear can be made very accurately such as this set made by *J Grainger's* for HMS Mersey to a set of model maker's drawings by Jacobin, **Photo 21.1**. A listing of manufactures can be found in Appendix 3.

When fitting the propeller tube the preliminary entry into the hull is both widened and lengthened depending on the angle of entry and position of the electric motors. Experience dictates that the motors are sited approximately one third of the length from the transom. Equally the length of any shaft must take into account the length of the coupling. There is no exact formula for this but allowances must be made for that mentioned above when making or ordering the running gear. Many warships are designed with a system for supporting the propeller end of the shaft called an "A" frame, **Photo 21.2**. The drawings usually indicate the exact position on the side elevation and through a section from a position on the body plan.

With the propeller tube fitted (at the correct angle) the "A" frame can also be slotted into place. To enable both shafts and "A" frames to align, a jig can be made that supports the shafts and maintains a correct alignment as per the drawing see **Photo 21.3**. At this stage the outer tube and "A" frame can be spot bonded into place with 5 minute 2 part epoxy. When this has set, filler can be applied around the propeller tube and "A" frame.

Above 23.1 Typical of the size of motors readily available.

Left 23.2 Triple 540 size motors.

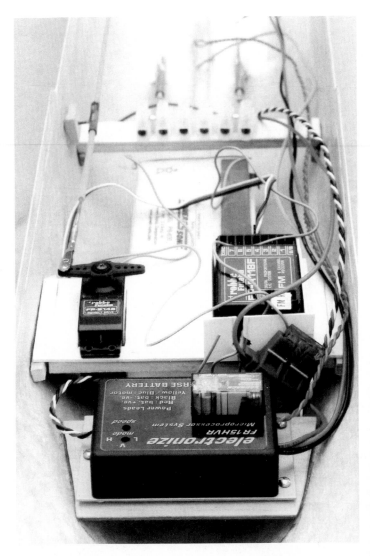

22.3 Radio receiver servo and electronic speed sontroller are grouped together.

The rudders and rudder linkages - Photo Series 22

The next stage includes the fitting of the rudderposts and rudders. Once again a simple jig can be made to maintain both the correct angle in relationship to the hull and the drawing as applied to the twin rudder model of HMS Mersey, **Photo 22.1**.

With the rudders in place and the rudder horns fitted, the linkages that connect each of the rudders together is fitted and the rudders are then linked via a push rod to a servo that is usually sited well forward or where the deck/superstructure lifts clear, **Photo 22.2**. Here the push rod is guided through a plastic tube in a direct line and secured via brass tubes to the inside of the hull. This is followed by the fitting of the battery tray, which is made in such a way that the selected battery can slide fore and aft to assist in trimming of the hull.

The servo, receiver and speed controller can be grouped in one place, allowing for as much unobstructed access as possible as, for example, the servo arm may need to be adjusted and the receiver crystal may need to be changed **Photo 22.3**.

Motors, their selection and installation - Photo Series 23

Most of the so-called "can" motors, which are at the inexpensive end of the motor range, such as the 385 or equivalent operate at between 6 and 12 volts and are ideally suited to powering smaller warship models of up to 1 metre such as the *Fleetscale* HMS Mersey. **Photo 23.1** gives some idea of the physical size of these motors although the motor on the right is a German Buhler, possessing a fairly high

24.1 Bilge keel as fitted to the FFG USS Donald B Beary.

torque and suitable for much larger models. The motors in the middle of the picture, particularly the 545 type are low drain and capable of powering hulls of up to 60in length and 8in beam. Three of these were used to power a model of the KM Blucher, which in turn was based on the *Fleetscale* GRP hull of the Prinz Eugen, **Photo 23.2**.

For HMS Mersey, 2 *MFA* motors were used both equivalent to the 385 which are supplied complete with motor mount and are easily fitted into place.

Not all commercial motors come with a dedicated mounting, as do those shown above and the shape of the hull may be more rounded dictating a more flexible type of mounting. **Photo 23.3** shows an example of motors developed by *Deans Marine* for their range of large models but used here to power the scratch built Russian armoured cruiser Rurik. The mounting is made so that it can be adjusted in

two planes to take into account the angle of the shaft and the curve of the hull. This is achieved by using bolts, which are adjusted until the mounting and motor are seated correctly in the hull. It will be noted that the coupling is in fact double universal. If the motor is aligned correctly then a single universal as shown on Mersey will be sufficient.

Bilge keels - Photo Series 24

With all the internal hardware in place the bilge keels can be fitted. These assist in maintaining stability in the rolling plane and can be seen on the FFG USS Donald Beary, fitted to the round of the bilge: note the stabiliser fin, **Photo 24.1**.

To make up the bilge keel first transfer, length and width from the profile and body plan to either wood, plastic or metal. The shape when flat should be rounded at each end. Using a pin vice, drill a series of four holes approximately 3mm deep into the bilge form **Photo 24.2** and bond brass rods approximately 15mm in length into place, **Photo 24.3**.

23.3 A fully adjustable mounting in any plane that conforms to the internal shape of the hull.

The entire shape is "thumb" bent to correspond with the shape on the profile drawing and offered into position. It will be noticed that where the "pins" strike the hull holes of corresponding size can be made. Remove excess length from the pins leaving approximately 5mm exposed inside the hull. This done the bilge keel can be fitted into place with adhesive being applied to each pin within the hull. When set, the final phase is to give the bilge keel its characteristic "wedge" shape. This is achieved by applying a layer of fillers

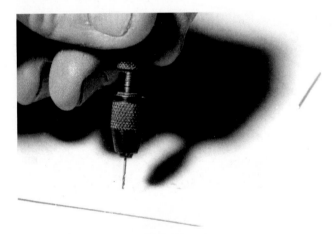

24.2 Using a pin vice to carefully drill into the edge of the bilge keel.

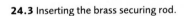

24.3 Inserting the brass securing rod.

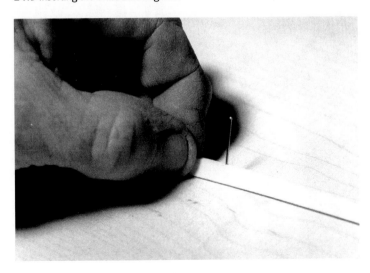

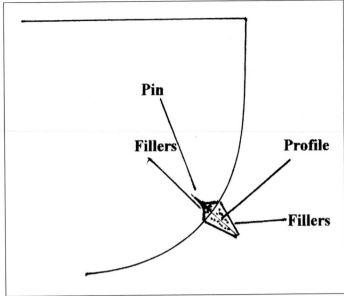

Fig 24.1 Section to show bilge keel construction.

24.4 The bilge keel profile set in place with fillers forming the wedge shape.

along the top and underside of the keel (**Fig 24.1**). When set this can be gently sanded down with medium wet and dry abrasive, **Photo 24.4**.

Wiring up ready for a test sail - Photo Series 25

Nothing is more confusing than having a "rat's nest" of wiring in a model. This leads to confusion when wiring and if any maintenance is required. Tracing the track of each wire and what that wire supplies is important and not a question of "out of sight out of mind". As the installation becomes more involved such as with the inclusion of pumps for water ballasting, bow thrusters or lighting, the internal arrangements need to be well marked and traceable. A good example of a "neat" installation can be seen in this model of the RFA replenishment ship Gold Rover by Paul Youde, **Photo 25.1**. This model uses a single electric Buhler motor for main power and a series of pumps for filling an on-board trim tank plus small bow thrusters forward. All of the wiring and switches need to be clearly marked. Equally the wiring needs to be grouped into "looms" and trunked even on simple installations so that it does not interfere with general maintenance.

25.1 A neat installation in a model of the RFA Gold Rover.

26.1 Trimming out before the deck and superstructure are fitted into place.

Test sailing and trimming - Photo Series 26

Once all the wiring is completed only then is it right to set the model on the water to ensure that the complete installation does not then hold any surprises when the deck and superstructure are in place. More importantly, ballasting can be carried out without the encumbrance of a superstructure as most lightweight superstructures have very little effect on the overall ballasting. If the superstructure is very high, then there may be a windage problem. Similarly, if there is a large number of metal or solid resin fittings above the water line these again may need to be taken into account even at this early stage. The battery used may well provide sufficient ballast without adding extra weight. However should further weight be required, then the open hull allows maximum freedom of action. Also it's worth considering the fact that weight, as in full size practice, is not all sited at the lowest point but placed up the side of the hull and just below the waterline, in what are termed "roll tanks". In effect this reduces the stiffness of the roll. On a model strip lead sited up the side of the hull allows the roll reaction to be similar to that of full size ship. As stated the battery can be adjusted as a controller of trim in the fore and aft plane - more on this later.

Once the hull is correctly trimmed work can commence on the deck and superstructure, **Photo 26.1**

Other choices

There are other methods that can be used to overcome problems related to the size of the model and the difficulties of transport. Take for example the 1:144 model of the Graf Zeppelin. Even at this small scale the hull measures over 70in length. Joseph Kovaks, a Canadian model builder, has solved this problem by dividing the hull into two separate sections that are bolted together as in **Photo 26.2** The joint is watertight and very difficult to see.

A further departure from the norm is in this 1:48 steam-powered model of the light cruiser HMS Chatham. Instead of an electric power plant, with its attendant problems, a steam plant has been fitted. Space is at a premium and such an installation requires a high degree of care when installing

26.2 A ship of two halves. A useful method to help with transport and internal installation.

26.3 A Steam powered HMS Chatham.

boiler and drive train, **Photo 26.3**. The butane gas tank is sited forward followed by the boiler with the steam engine just out of the picture, however it will be noted that the entire deck is removable to provide maximum access.

Batteries

Apart from the example shown above there are few warship models powered by steam. Most are electric and by implication require a power supply in the form of batteries.

There is a wide range available and choice is broadly dependent on the size of the model and the motors in use. However for general use and availability there are two specific types. Those types of batteries that are listed as "gel" cells, sealed lead acid batteries that require a charger of a constant voltage, and NiCad cells requiring a constant current charger.

The gel cell is a lead acid type, sealed but vented. A single cell from a sealed lead acid battery is rated at 2.0 volts. The most common battery voltage is either 12 or 6v. These batteries were originally designed for standby power systems such as emergency lighting. In simple terms if a motor propeller combination draws 2 Amps, a 10AH cell could sustain that discharge for up to 5 hours.

The 7.2volts NiCad pack is a familiar type used in model cars and comprises 6 cells each of 1.2volts. Like the gel cell, the NiCad capacity can vary depending on the physical size of each cell but the voltage per cell does remain constant although can vary depending on the discharge rate and the condition of the cell. The capacity of a NiCad can vary from as little as 250mAh right through to 10Ah and the more cells added to the pack the greater the voltage. Although as a word of warning, all the cells in a pack must be of the same capacity. For example if each cell is rated at 2Ah then all the cells within that pack must be rated at 2Ah. It is unwise to allow a NiCad pack to run completely flat during a sailing session.

It is often quoted that NiCads suffer from memory. If possible to avoid the problem of residual capacity and to maintain a full charge capacity cycle, occasionally discharge each cell individually till a meter reading shows just below 1v. Then slowly recharge the pack as if it were new at the supplier's recommended rate. Most commercial NiCad chargers can operate at this rate, usually 50mAH. Some NiCad chargers are fitted with sensors that automatically close down the charge when the cells are fully charged and are often designed for fast and slow trickle charging.

26.4 A 7.2v NiCad pack ideal for small models.

27.1 Styrene used to form the camber of the deck.

27.2 When cutting styrene it does well to use a safety rule.

27.3 The fitting of a styrene deck on the OPV HMS Mersey.

In general kit manufactures have seen the advantage of the 7.2v NiCad battery pack and have recommended this as standard. An example of this philosophy can be seen in **Photo 26.4** of the internal arrangement of a *Deans Marine* HMS Amazon. Once again the battery can move fore and aft within the confines of the tray.

Preparation for the deck and superstructure - Photo Series 27

With water trials successfully completed, the next stage is to build in the gunwale stringer and bearers. The following really only need apply to those building from a GRP hull as a scratch built hull will have many of these supports in place in the form of the bulkheads.

Following on from the preparation outlined in Chapter 5 Photo Series 15, the next stage is to cut to size and fit the deck beams, which should be sited relative to any openings in the deck. Accompanying the deck beams are plastic strips cut to the camber of the deck. These may need to be adjusted depending on the deflection of the camber from the stem through to the stern, **Photo 27.1**. Note that the stringer is the thickness of the deck below the top of the hull.

With all the deck beams and cambers in place, the deck surface can be cut from either wood or plastic. Just a word of caution when choosing plastic for this purpose. It must be judged by area; the greater the area of plastic used for a sub-deck or deck, the greater the potential for distortion due to changes in temperature. This was experienced on Moskva. At its worst the deck could lose its integrity and separate from the bearers. Plastic sheet for deck covering should be kept to the minimum. HMS Mersey is about the largest conveniently sized deck that can be used without exposing the plastic to the problems outlined above. Equally decks should be compatible with the surface they are to be bonded to; wood bearers/wooden deck, plastic bearers/plastic deck. Although there are adhesives such as *De-Luxe Materials* R/C Modellers Glue that allow styrene and wood to be bonded with confidence.

Plastic or styrene is an excellent material to use and offers an ideal surface for paint; this will be discussed in Chapter 9. Cutting styrene is easy but as with any material basic care needs to be considered. Always use a sharp blade in the modelling knife and it helps to use a "safety rule" similar to that shown in **Photo 27.2**. Here the deck has been marked out and is being cut to size. The deck is then offered into place and trimmed where necessary to give a snug fit. This procedure can be used regardless of the type of model or shape of GRP hull. With the deck seated correctly all is prepared for permanently bonding the deck into the hull, **Photo 27.3**. With the main deck in place, initial sea trials over and confident with the internal installation, thoughts can shift to the building of the superstructure.

Chapter Seven

Techniques for building superstructure and turrets

Superstructure, bridges and armoured towers - Photo Series 28

Having put the main deck in place and satisfactorily installed and tested all the internal hardware, the next step is to start building up the superstructure. As in previous chapters a GRP hull of the OPV HMS Mersey will be used to explain and give a number of specific examples of the methods involved. Although styrene has been used to illustrate the basic principles, where appropriate alternative materials such as timber and metal will be used.

The shape of the superstructure can be difficult to interpret from a one-dimensional drawing. Photographs are without doubt one of the best aids to interpreting the structure that develops into the shape seen in the drawing. For the modeller the main concern is to develop the shape or series of shapes without too much concern for the internals, although as we shall see these can become a factor.

The bridge

The main consideration is the arrangement of the internal supports and also the methods that can be used to build a particular type of mast as in some instances the mast and the superstructure form part of the same structure. Take for example **Photo 28 1**, the Sovremennyy class DDG, which shows the structure abaft of the fore mast and compare this with **Photo 28 2**. It's hard to believe that one of these pictures is in fact a model but can you guess which one?

This highlights the need for good information when building up such complex structures. By contrast there are relatively straightforward structures that are almost box like. An example of this can be seen in **Photo 28.3**, a large 1:72 superstructure for a USN LPH which has relatively few

28.1 The complex mast structure seen on a Sovremennyy class DDG.

28.2 Sovremennyy DDG "Model or the real thing"?

28.5 North Carolina as a preserved warship.

difficult sections to take into account.

Photo 28.4 shows a 1:96 USS North Carolina by Ron Horabin with a superstructure built up using a combination of balsa, 0.5mm ply and litho plate. It is interesting to note that the original is now a Museum ship with much of the wartime detailing remaining in place, **Photo 28.5**.

Main armoured tower of a 1:128 KM Blucher - Photo Series 29

The shapes are transferred from the drawing to the chosen material in a similar manner to that used for creating the

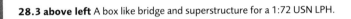

28.3 above left A box like bridge and superstructure for a 1:72 USN LPH.

29.1 below Part of the bridge assembly for a 1:128 KM Blucher.

29.3 left Each one of the sections forming part of the armoured tower are interlocking.

28.4 bottom One piece detachable superstructure on a 1:96 USS North Carolina.

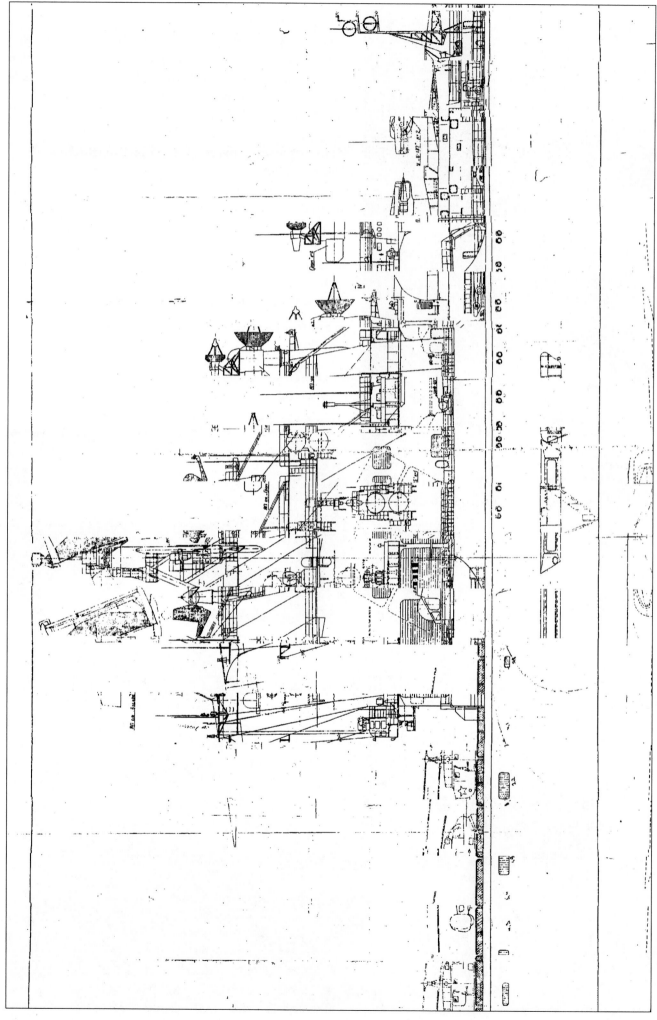

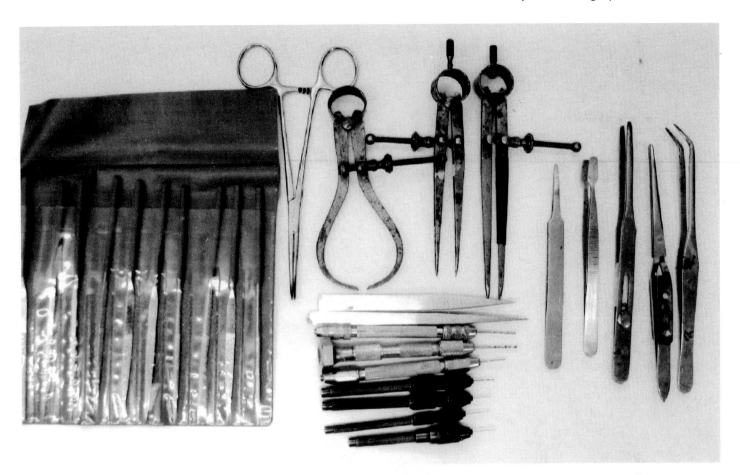

30.1 Useful tools like pin vices and various sizes of tweezers.

difficult sections to take into account.

Main armoured tower of a 1:128 KM Blucher - Photo Series 29

The shapes are transferred from the drawing to the chosen material in a similar manner to that used for creating the bulkhead templates. Styrene is such a versatile material that fairly complex shapes can be formed such as the lower half of the bridge on the heavy cruiser Blucher seen here in Photo 29.1 and in its entirety prior to painting in Photo 29.2 (see colour section). The rounded tower that supports all the platforms is made from balsa (to reduce top weight) and is sheathed with 0.010in styrene sheet. The bonding agent for styrene to balsa is the aforementioned R/C Modeller's Glue. It will be noted in Photo 29.1 that there are two plastic rods of 2mm diameter rising up from the bridge platform. These are in fact locating pins for locking all the platforms to the following sections of the tower.

When building a 1:96 model of Tirpitz, these rods were made from 4BA, threaded mild steel rod (studding) with one rod commencing at the base of the tower and terminating at the very top where the small platform for the rangefinder is sited. The purpose of which was to allow this part of the model the freedom of not being bonded to each of the lower

Fig 30.1 GA drawing used to build the Soviet aviation cruiser Moskva.

sections. Thus a gentle tightening of the top nut effectively locked all the components of the armoured tower together. The rationale being that in the unlikely event that the main tower was damaged, the entire unit could be separated without destroying other parts of the structure. The armoured tower of the Blucher may look complex but it's really a series of platforms from the main superstructure right through to the top of the tower. **Photo 29.3** shows the completed armoured tower. Interestingly the funnel casing is made up of a ply framework covered with a sheet of 0.010in litho plate bonded to the inner frame using epoxy resin.

Building the superstructure on the aviation cruiser Moskva - Photos Series 30

The following series of photos deals with the more complicated shape inherent in the Soviet aviation cruiser Moskva. Not having encountered such a complex form before, it became necessary to accumulate as much information as possible before any serious consideration could be given to the construction. As described in Chapter 3, photos are the prime sources in clarifying those areas aboard the vessel that drawings alone are simply unable to do.

For this very unusual subject, publications such as "Soviet Warships" by John Jordan and the Polish publication "Okrety Lotnicze Rosji" by Wladimir Zablocki (see Bibliography, Appendix 2). Both publications included outline drawings and photos of both Moskva and her sister ship Leningrad. The plans used for the model were of Russian origin and an example of the superstructure is shown in **Fig 30.1**.

This model was built in the late 1990s and I will be the

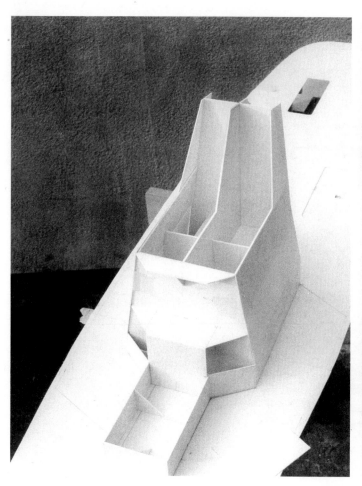

30.2 The internal supports for the main superstructure on Moskva.

30.3 Much thought went into developing the constructional shapes required to follow the plan accurately.

31.1 The OPV HMS Mersey P283. Many of the structural shapes were unique to the class.

31.2 Building up the sides of the superstructure on Mersey.

31.4 The bridge and roof were cast in resin. To reduce weight the roof was made in styrene.

first to admit to the errors made in the choice of materials, or more importantly, the quantity of a single material, mainly 0.040in styrene sheet. Do bear in mind the previous comments warning of stability problems where large areas of styrene sheet are used.

Nonetheless, styrene exhibits qualities that few other materials can match. One example is that joints are "welded" with a strength factor equal to the material as a whole. Thus, used wisely, it is the ideal medium for the complex shapes inherent in the Moskva design. As a matter of interest, the use of angled plates and sharp edges is now well known as an effective method of reducing radar cross section. It is worth pausing for thought to consider that the original design of the Moskva goes back to the late 1950s, long before the so called progressive "western" navies incorporated radar reflective features on their warships.

Building up the superstructure with styrene sheet
Following the same procedures with regard to cutting the deck shape from 0.030in styrene sheet as discussed in Chapter 6 the material of choice could equally have been

31.3 Cross members are put in place to give lateral strength.

0.04 or 0.08mm ply. The tools required at this stage are relatively few and include a straight and curved edge craft knife, finger sander, a sanding block, various sanding strips plus an assortment of wet and dry paper for rubbing down surfaces. A general selection of small tools which includes needle files, dividers, locking forceps, assortment of tweezers and pin vices with various sizes of drill bits fitted will be useful, **Photo 30.1**.

Apart from the above list of tools a more flexible friend for the model maker is filler; either green putty or "Plasto". . The usefulness of these materials cannot be exaggerated, as not all joints will be "perfect".

The superstructure elements for Moskva were lifted from the plan, profile and foreword elevation and the results of the early stages of assembly of the main superstructure can be judged. The styrene was bonded using a liquid polystyrene cement that is actually a solvent and melts the surface of the plastic. *Humbrol* Liquid Poly or any plastic solvent adhesive should be used as per the instructions and to achieve the best results "irrigate" the joint using a fine brush, as an excessive amount of solvent can actually have a detrimental effect on the plastic. This can be a major factor for the thinner styrene.

The following series of photos give some idea of the methodology used in building the styrene superstructure on Moskva.

Photo 30.2 illustrates how the inner shape mirrors the side profiles yet the actual side plates are angled inward. Note also that at this early stage, the hanger/garage area at deck level is modelled into the structure with the top of the stack following a profile to conform to the unusual shape seen in **Photo 30.3**. Again all the styrene surfaces are welded using Liquid Poly. Note the critical angles cut to conform to the shape abaft of the stack. First cutting and fitting the sloped back from 0.030in sheet, followed by inserting the exact "V" with the edges slightly chamfered allowing the form to comfortably marry with the sloped angle of the stack.

31.5 The complex shape of the mast as fitted to HMS Mersey.

31.6 A mast made of styrene.

Completed structure on Moskva

Interestingly, it will be noted that the sides at deck level surrounding the main superstructure, are in fact slightly cambered and fixed into place, whilst the superstructure remains completely removable **Photo 30.4** (see colour section). Along with this main structure, the forward deck housings are also built up and they follow the distinctive form of sloping surfaces.

The forward section, which houses the SAN-3 launchers, was permanently secured when the forward deck and deck housings were given their final coating of paint which will be discussed in Chapter 9. Compare this with the near-completed superstructure. The mast surmounting the top of the stack, which supports the large "Top Sail" 3D radar, is detachable and made up from brass tube. The pillars that support all of the radar arrays are 5mm "Evergreen" plastic tube, again more on this later, **Photo 30.5** (see colour section).

The method of building up the superstructure on HMS Mersey - Photo Series 31

Chapter 5 described how the hull was prepared and the deck fitted on a 1:96 scale HMS Mersey. Moving on to the next phase of the build of this 35in OPV, **Photo 31.1** shows for the first time how the full size vessel appears.

With the deck in place, the next step is to build up the combing around the inside of the opening into the hull. Once again styrene is the material of choice. With the combing in place the sides of the superstructures can be cut to size and seated around the outside. Care must be taken to ensure that no solvent comes into contact with the raised combing as this part of the build is permanently fixed to the deck, whilst the sides of the superstructure must be free to be lifted clear. But in the initial stages pegs or small clamps can be used to ensure that the sides of the superstructure maintain a good fit, **Photo 31.2**. Note that angle stiffeners are used to reinforce the corners. Also, the camber of the weather decks needs to be accounted for as this is shown in the drawing

and in photographs of the full size vessel.

At this early stage in construction the sides, without any internal supports, are inherently weak and could break up if prematurely lifted clear. In order that the newly formed superstructure becomes more rigid, an internal framework of styrene is built up. This can be seen in **Photo 31.3**. This method can be applied to any warship model where there are raised combings surrounding openings through the deck, and by implication form a major part of the superstructure.

Equally timber could have been used for the deck and the raised combings, as was the case on the model of Blucher. There is no hard and fast rule governing the selection of materials. In fact timber used in this way would have provided a better former for the building up of the sides in styrene, as the solvent used during the building of the superstructure would have had no effect on a timber combing.

When dry the framework that now forms the lower half of the superstructure can be lifted clear. With the aid of 3in dividers the deck (now referred to as 01 Deck), can be accurately marked onto a suitably sized sheet of 0.030in styrene by transferring the measurements from the top of the newly formed framework.

Resin castings are frequently employed to provide parts of the superstructures of warship models by manufacturers, (usually the bridge area either for kits or semi-scratch models) and Mersey is no exception. This of course can be hand made but a bridge cast from resin does save some time particularly if there are a large number of windows needing to be formed. Accompanying this resin cast bridge was a solid resin roof, which was a little on the weighty side.

In order to reduce some unnecessary top weight, the roof can be fabricated and when fitted into place will match the resin original at only 1/3 of the weight. Styrene for all its limitations is without doubt a versatile material and this was borne out when building up the exhaust stack and the mast. Both contain, like those of the Moskva, some complex shapes, note the bridge roof in place, **Photo 31.4**.

The drawing of the mast for HMS Mersey provided views

33.1 The turret on a 1:48 HMS Devastation.

32.1 The Bridge Joseph Kaisers superb 1:100 scale Bismarck.

32.2 The same subject as Photo 32.1 but this bridge and armoured tower is made entirely from brass sheet and soldered up. *(Photo Author's collection)*

Above 33.2 A 6in breech loading gun.

Right 33.3 Resin cast 5in/38 at 1:96 scale.

34.1 Forming the shape of the Soviet 57mm in gellutong timber for the Moskva.

Below 33.4 The 5inch/38 calibre gun fitted to DD-661 USS Kidd.

from various elevations but where possible these need to be supplemented by photographs. **Photo 31.5. Photo 31.6** shows the completed styrene mast ready for painting. Cyanoacrylate or super glue can be used but does not weld the styrene. Nonetheless, cyanoacrylate is a useful adhesive and is ideal for bonding many of the metal parts to styrene. This stage of the construction is now complete and the superstructure is ready to accept the various fittings such as WT, doors, ladders, and vents etc some of which shall be discussed in the following chapter.

Styrene turrets - Photo Series 35

Apart from resin and timber a turret can be built up from styrene, which is both light and almost ready to accept paint. This series of photos illustrate the build sequence.

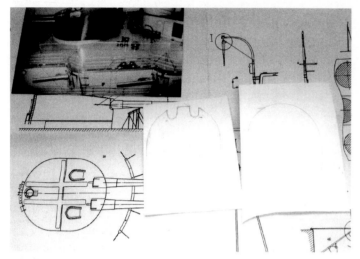

35.1 Depending on the shape and type of turret the base and top are marked out.

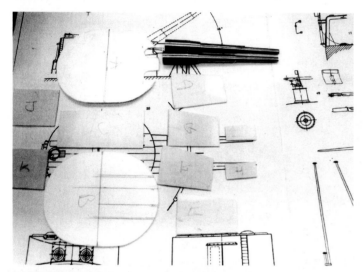

35.2 All the internal parts are cut to size and shape and are marked in sequence A-B and so on.

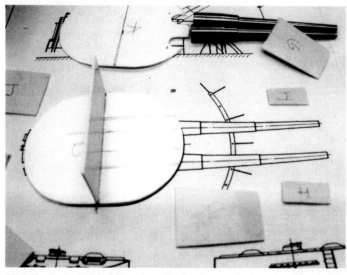

35.3 The centre support frame is set in place.

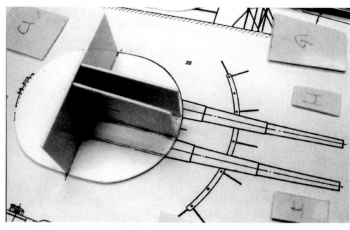

35.4 Each of the centre pair of four sides supporting the internal part of the barrel are bonded to the centre frame and base.

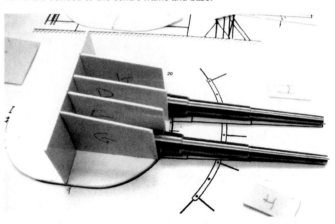

35.5 The outer barrel supports are fitted. Note either side of the barrels a small section, which is fitted between each barrel support to ensure a pre-determined angle of elevation.

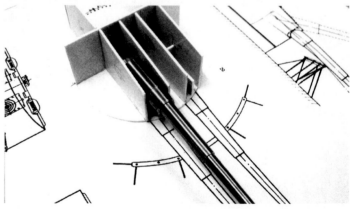

35.6 Each barrel is slotted into place ensuring a good fit at the right angle.

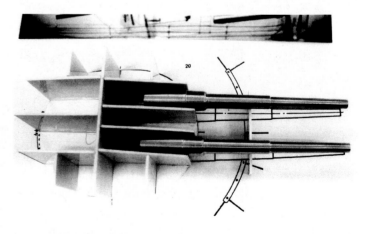

35.7 The remainder of the internal supports around the outer edge of the turret are fitted.

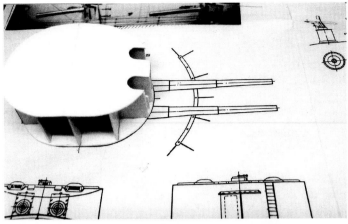

35.8 A cut is made in the roof allowing this to follow the slope of the forward part of the turret.

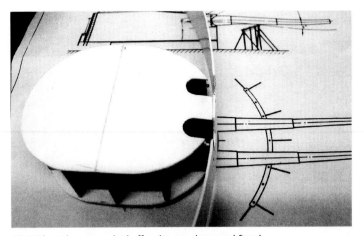

35.9 The sides are marked off and cut to shape and fitted.

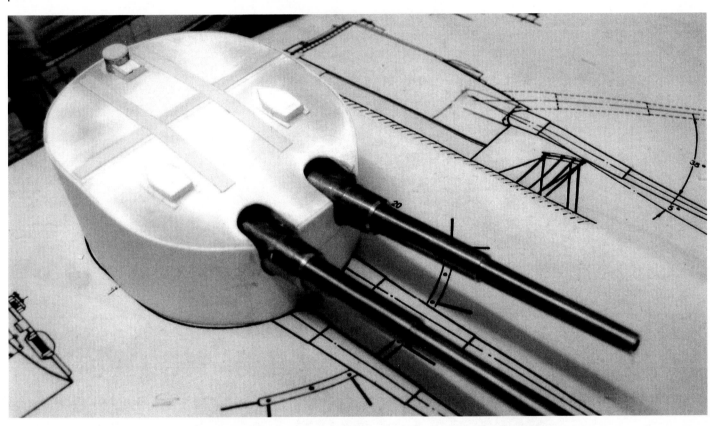

35.10 & 11 above and right
Any additional features are added like rangefinders, periscopes, ladders and doors.

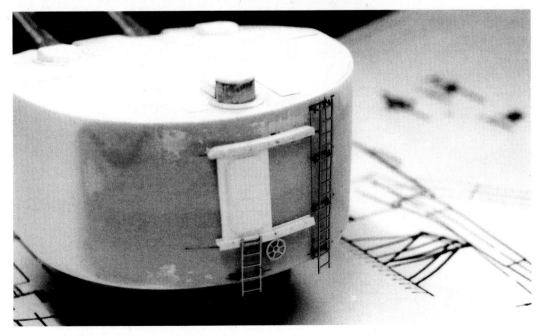

36.3 The main lattice mast on the FFG Stephen Groves.

Bismarck - a superstructure in metal - Photo Series 32

Joseph Kaiser from Germany has built what is probably one of the finest examples of the battleship Bismarck and the attention to detail in this 1:100 model is stunning, **Photo 32.1**. However this leads me on to describe another method of construction, which is both versatile and in many respects far superior to styrene. **Photo 32.2** shows the forward superstructure, similar to that in **Photo 32.1** for a 1:72 Bismarck initially prepared by Andrei Gorbunnov, a manufacturer of model ships in Russia, using brass as the material of choice. The sheet brass is first etched and comes as a flat pack, which is folded precisely and soldered along the joints.

Turrets - Photo Series 33

Turrets are, and will remain part of the weapons fit of the warship for the foreseeable future. The turret has evolved considerably since the end of WW2 but in model form it remains the "piece de resistance" of any warship even from the early days of the so-called turret ship and can be seen here fitted to a model of the turret ship HMS Devastation at 1:48. Most of the early big guns like these 12in, 35 ton weapons as fitted to Devastation were in fact muzzle loaded, **Photo 33.1**. Eventually the big gun evolved to a breech-loaded weapon, similar to that in **Photo 33.2**. Armoured turrets were to follow enclosing all of the breech and giving protection for those inside, see Chapters 1 and 2. These evolved into formidable weapons such as this triple 16in on the preserved battleship USS North Carolina.

Turrets can be made using a variety of methods and the finished results are illustrated well on this commercial solid cast-resin turret for a 5inch/38 mounting (**Photo 33.3**) at 1:96. These guns were fitted to destroyers such as the "Fletcher" class, preserved destroyer DD661 USS Kidd, **Photo 33.4**.

Fabricating turrets in timber and Styrene - Photo Series 34

One of the simplest ways to make a turret having a shape with both rounded and flat surfaces, such as this Soviet 57mm at 1:125 as fitted to Moskva, is to model in gelutong, a close-grained, pattern maker's timber, which can be very easily shaped to present sharp corners and a clean rounded surface. An example of the basic turret cut and sanded to shape can be seen in Photo **34.1**. The timber form can be treated with a sanding sealer, sanded down and either sprayed with Hi-Build primer (see Chapter 9) or further coats of sanding sealer applied until the grain is merged into a complete smooth surface. The various fittings such as access doors etc.; cut and shaped from either styrene or litho plate can then be fitted. Like the "Sovremenny" class the barrels are water-cooled and although brass tube is used for the barrel, the water cooling pipes can be simulated by using flexible copper wire.

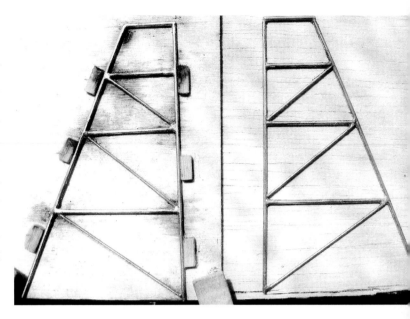

36.2 both left and right sections of the mast for a Krivak 1 are soldered up in a jig.

36.4 With the soldering completed the tape removed the completed mast is removed from the profile.

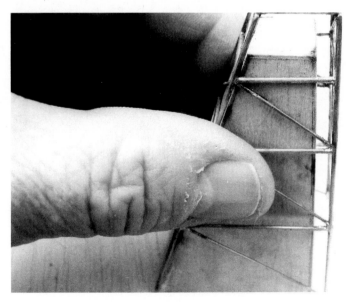

Masts on modern warships and methods of construction for the modeller (Photo Series 36) FFG USS Stephen Groves

Apart from the cage masts fitted to many early USN "Dreadnought" battleships, lattice masts come close to being amongst the most taxing form to construct. An example of this can be seen in **Photo 36.1** showing the masts as fitted to the FFG USS Stephen Groves supporting the SPS 49 air search radar and the main mast with the TACAN at the mast head.

Using tracing paper lift the shape from the profile or mast drawing. Then transfer the tracing to a small sheet of timber. The brass tube or rod that form the side supports and cross framing can be cut to size. These are then mounted on the timber conforming to the pre-marked profile, and the cross supports are soldered into place, **Photo 36.2**. This is repeated for each side. A 3D timber profile is made conforming to the inside measurements of the mast and the soldered form is then taped to this profile. Using low temperature solder and heat sinks, the cross members are soldered in place. With the soldering completed and tape removed, the mast can be eased clear of the profile, **Photo 36.4**.

Chapter Eight

Fittings, etched work and castings

Fittings, etched work and castings - Photo Series 37

With the bulk of the superstructure prepared, thoughts can move to the type of fittings that need to be used. Of course this is a generalisation as the question that can be posed is what constitutes a fitting? As modellers, our interest broadly speaking concerns those parts of the ship clearly visible to the eye. For example guns of all types, deck hatches (a description that usually encompasses any opening into the spaces below), cranes, radars, aircraft, ladders, stairways, railings; the list can go on. But the real need for the modeller is "how to"? In previous chapters references have been made to what could be the accepted divisions of model building into kit, semi-scratch and scratch-built. Kits generally include all of the fittings needed and prepared plans and instructions directing the modeller to the exact location of the fitting on the model and all the preparation needed for installation.

37.1 Scratch built fittings for a 1:48 HMS Starling.

Should the alternative of a GRP hull and plan set be chosen, many of the essential fittings to accompany the hull can be purchased as and when needed. The alternative is to make every fitting from scratch. An example can be seen in the fittings for a 1:48 model of HMS Starling by Ted Parr shown in **Photo 37.1**.

Apart from fittings manufactured in resin, white metal and brass etched frets are commonly found. The latter usually accounts for items such as stanchions, hand wheels, WT doors, and in some cases, delicate items such as radar arrays.

Photographs of a particular fitting or group of fittings on the full-size ship are an invaluable tool for the modeller. A photograph helps not only to identify the shape of the fitting but also its exact location in relationship to other fittings. But more importantly for the modeller the time frame in which the picture was taken (see Chapter 3). Many official plans are either "as fitted" or prepared before construction began and do not necessarily represent the vessel "as modelled". The knowledge gained from date stamped photos can be applied across the board regardless whether the model is from a kit, semi-kit or scratch-built.

Reworking stock fittings

A good example of this basic principle can be gained from the *Deans Marine* 1:96 model of the RN Hydrographic vessel HMS Bulldog shown in **Photo 37.2**. Photographic material can verify beyond doubt how the ship appeared at a particular point in time and that evidence applied to enhance what is essentially quite a basic kit. Naturally not all modellers feel that they need to alter the original kit but a kit can be viewed as either an end in itself or an opportunity for improvement. Either way many of the fittings supplied in a kit or those

37.2 Hydrographic survey vessels HMS Bulldog, June 1998.

37.3 Reflecting changes to the boat arrangement.

38.1 A 1:128 HMS Hood circa 1923.

bought separately for a semi-kit can be improved up on.

Apart from alterations to the colour scheme during the period that Bulldog was in RN service, other functional changes occurred that altered the outer appearance. For example, the kit provides fittings particularly those relating to the ships boats which present Bulldog as built in 1968. However pictures taken in March 1998 indicate alterations to the boat arrangement on the port side, **Photo 37.2** and this was reflected in the completed model, **Photo 37.3**. This stresses the importance of photos and making use of a time frame, as fittings and their positions can change. Photos are an invaluable tool that can be used to advantage to give stock fittings provided in the kit a more authentic appearance.

Ships boats on HMS Hood - Photo Series 38
A time frame is important and placing the correct fitting in the correct place is essential to give authenticity to a model. An example of this can be seen in Steve Leek's 1:128 model of HMS Hood dressed overall for the 1923 World Cruise. This particular layout reflects HMS Hood in her near-original state, which is seldom a modeller's first choice when dealing with this particular subject, **Photo 38.1**. In 1923 Hood carried two 50ft pinnaces and a smaller 45ft steam pinnace

secured close to the boat boom. The ship's boats that include whalers, cutters and the steam pinnace are of commercial manufacture, **Photo 38.2**. These particular resin moulded boats required very little remedial work in the way of removing the flash and, as can be seen in these photos, that little extra cost in time is well justified, (see Appendix 3).

WT doors - Photo Series 39
Wide ranges of fittings for the warship modeller are available from commercial sources such as *John Haynes*, *Sirmar*, and *Lee Upshaw*. Most reflect the original fitting well but others

38.2 An excellent commercially resin moulded 50 ft Steam Pinnace.

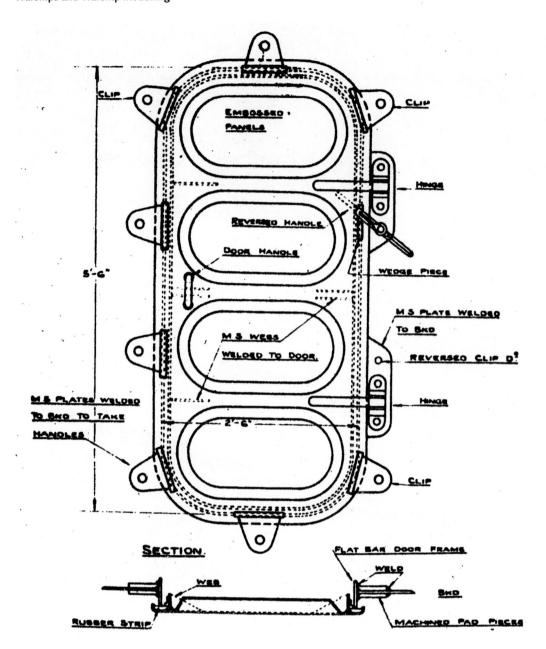

do require some additional work. Again one of the best ways to view the original is through photographs. Take for example watertight doors with **Fig 39.1** showing a typical embossed panel type common to many ships of the Royal Navy. Physically the door is 5ft 6in high by 2ft 6in wide and is provided with two hinges. It is secured by means of clips that can be operated from either side of the bulkhead, **Photo 39.1**. Compare this with a WT door as fitted to the "Arleigh Burke" class of DDGs, **Photo 39.2**. Included are a number of examples like those cast in resin, white metal and etched frets, **Photo 39.3**. Commercial standard WT doors are fitted to HMS Mersey and are far simpler than the RN embossed type, manufactured in resin form, the reverse side needs to be well trimmed in order to achieve the right thickness only then are the hinges and door handle fitted.

Davits - Photo Series 40

Other common items such as davits, are often cast in resin or white metal and examples can be seen here fitted to HMS Bulldog, **Photo 40.1**. All that is required to finish these is for the surface to be sanded down with wet and dry. Preparation of these fittings is minimal. By contrast those made by Ted Parr for his 1:48 "Starling". are all made from scratch, **Photo 40.2**. The davits to the left and right of the picture are for the 27ft sea boat and made from 0.010in brass see **Fig 40.1**. The 32ft cutter davits are made from brass rod. A davit made in this way can be relatively straightforward to construct. Depending on the scale, select the appropriate diameter brass rod mark the length from the drawing and cut to length. Using a small flat file, form a taper. Making use of a small plastic tube, bend the tapered end to form the curve of the davit. The next step depending on scale, is to drill a small hole at the end of the curve so that an eye plate for the davit guy and spreader jackstay can be inserted and provide a support for the cross head, see **Photo 40.3**. The cleat for the falls can now be cut and soldered into place, **Photo 40.4** & **Fig 40.2** with the supports for the gripping spar cut from lining tape along with the cross head for the boat falls.

A disengaging gear is usually fitted within the sea boat that allows the boat to be released simultaneously from each

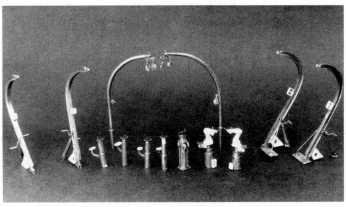

40.2 Scratch made davits for a 1:48 HMS Starling.

Fig 40.1 Typical of the type of davit fitted to many RN warships of WW2.

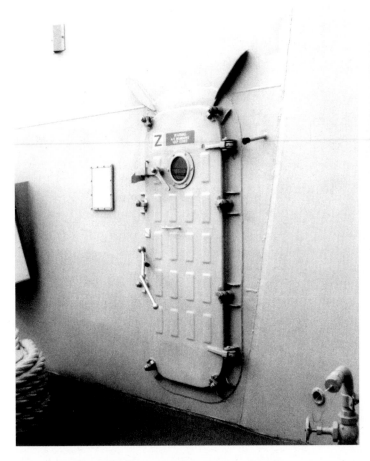

39.2 WT door as fitted to the Arleigh Burke class of DDGs.

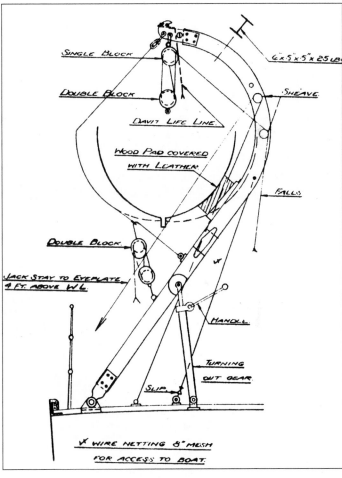

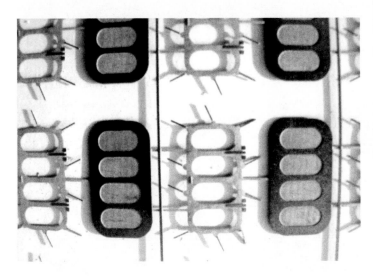

39.3 etched fret of RN embossed type WT doors.

of the boat falls, **Fig 40.3** and **Photo 40.5**.

Stanchions - Photo Series 41

Stanchions come in a variety of types some referred to as either three bar, four bars, flat, or round with solid rails or flexible rail like those fitted to the Type 23 class frigate HMS Richmond, **Photo 41.1**.

Over the years etched frets have made their mark particularly where stanchions are concerned. There are a number of methods used to reproduce stanchions or a run of rails that incorporates stanchions. The one single drawback

of this type of railing is the two dimensional effect which can detract from what is otherwise seen as a well-built model. It is worth remembering that bars or rails are generally neither flat nor continuous although some stanchions are quite flat, for example, those on HMS Mersey, **Photo 41.2**.

An etched fret is available from *Scale Link* (see Appendix 3) which accurately replicates those fitted to the Mersey. This is shown in **Photo 41.3** and like other types of stanchion or etched fitting it can be easily removed from the fret. I find it handy to use a curved blade with the fret placed on a discarded sheet of styrene. The plastic is hard enough to

39.1 above Typical of the type of WT door fitted to RN warships.

40.1 Commercially made davits.

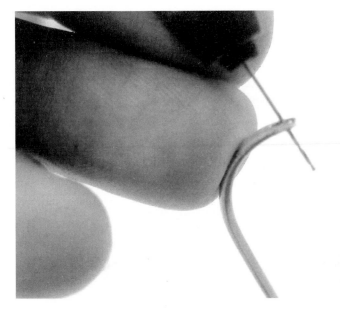

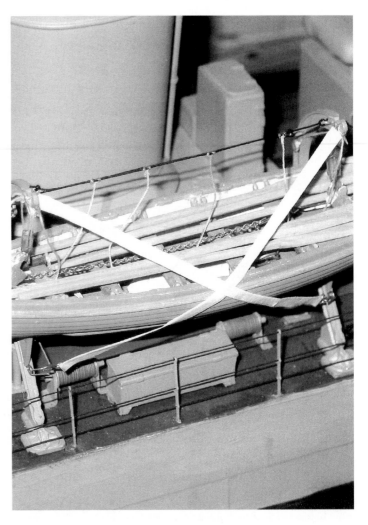

40.5 Disengaging gear as fitted to a 27 ft sea boat.

40.3 **above left** Using a pin vice to drill the end of davit for supporting the eye plate.

40.4 The basic davit including cleat for falls and cross head in place ready for sheaves.

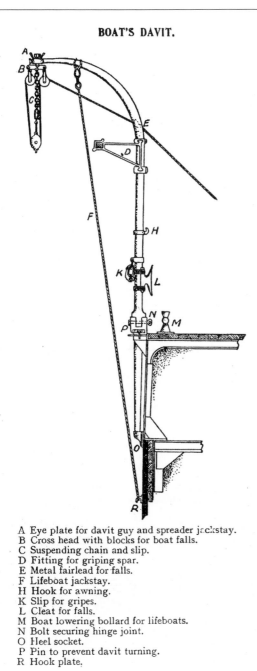

BOAT'S DAVIT.

A Eye plate for davit guy and spreader jackstay.
B Cross head with blocks for boat falls.
C Suspending chain and slip.
D Fitting for griping spar.
E Metal fairlead for falls.
F Lifeboat jackstay.
H Hook for awning.
K Slip for gripes.
L Cleat for falls.
M Boat lowering bollard for lifeboats.
N Bolt securing hinge joint.
O Heel socket.
P Pin to prevent davit turning.
R Hook plate.

Fig. 40.2 Parts of a davit.

allow the blade to cut accurately without distorting the item being cut from the fret however; the useful life of a sharp blade is quite limited.

Setting stanchions and rails into place

The positions of each of the stanchions are determined from the drawing and marked on the edge of the hull or superstructure. A pin vice can be used to hold a small drill for boring the locating hole for the stanchion, **Photo 41.4**. Once a number of stanchions have been inserted into place, (**Photo 41.5**) a length of 0.030in diameter brass wire is cut to form the top rail. The length of this depends on whether the bar has any tight curves. Should this be so, then it's expedient to cut at a point were the rail meets the first stanchion following the curve. If there is a continuation of that length onto another curve, then any straight rails need to be inserted into each stanchion before the next curved rail is put into place. Using this method any curve can be catered for and produce an almost invisible joint, **Photo 41.6**.

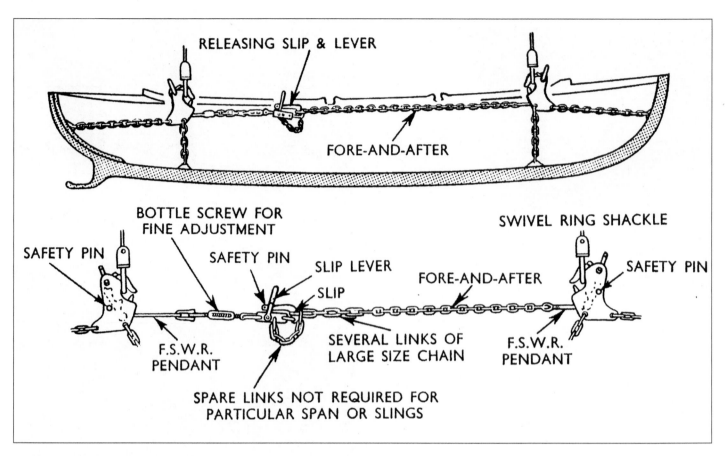

Fig 40.3 above Robinson's disengaging gear.

40.4 below The basic davit including cleat for falls and cross head in place ready for sheaves.

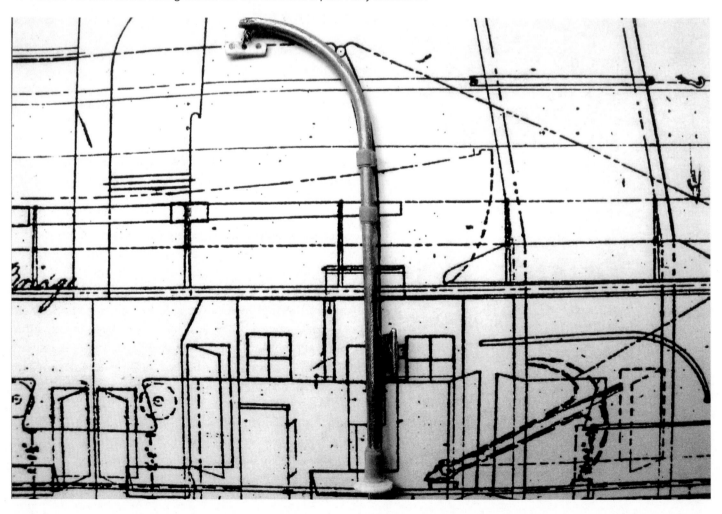

41.2 Flat profile 3 bar type stanchion fitted to HMS Mersey OPV Off Shore Patrol Vessel.

41.3 Etched flat profile type as fitted to HMS Mersey.

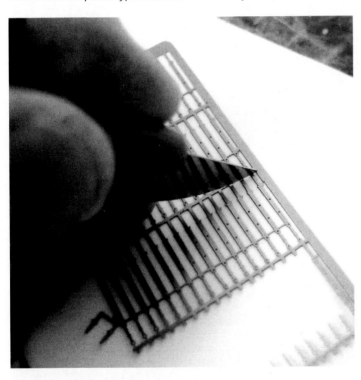

41.4 Preparation for fitting stanchions.

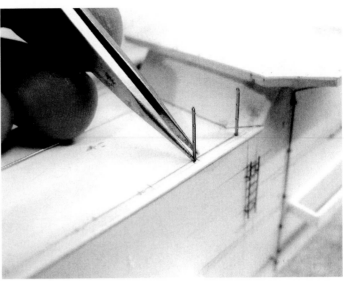

41.5 Setting each stanchion in place.

41.6 Fitting rails and forming double curves.

Making Stanchions from scratch - Photo Series 42

All the handrails are made from brass wire using a combination 0.030in for the stanchions and top bar whilst the second and third bars are from 0.015in. Each stanchion is cut to 0.5in longer than needed. The top bar is fitted into the jig and each of the stanchions "butt" soldered into place on the bar. The second and third bars laid across each of the stanchions secured to the jig and soldered. Using this simple jig and after a little practice a 12inch length can be completed in about ten minutes, **Photo 42.1**. Although the wire used is very fine the assembled length is quite robust and easily set into place. After trimming the excess from each of the stanchions, the completed length is set aside and the next length made ready and so on until about a dozen lengths have been prepared. These are then cleaned up in warm soapy water to remove any traces of flux used in soldering and are now ready for spraying. The results can be seen on the after section of the 1:128 KM Blucher, **Photo 42.2**.

119

41.1 Three ball RN type stanchions.

42.2 The finished results on Blucher .

Decks - Photo Series 43

It is generally accepted that on a full-size ship, deck planking fulfils two criteria; firstly appearance and secondly, to help maintain a tolerable temperature in the living spaces below.

Planks are usually laid parallel to the middle line, with a Borneo whitewood cutting plank next to the waterway following the run of the ship's side. It was standard practice for the waterway planking to be laid in teak. Common shipyard practice is to lay each of the planks well shifted with each other and the steel deck (4 planks to the butt). Planking can be either 7 or 5in wide and a thickness of 2-1/2in, with the planks being secured to the steel via studs welded to the plating. The joints are first sealed by forcing oakum (unravelled tarred cordage) into the joints, this followed by a marine glue pitch.

Laying deck planks

Begin by laying the margin planks around deck fittings, deck edges and barbettes. **Photo 43.1** shows margin planks in place. This is followed by the laying of the king plank on the centre line, usually from a point at the forecastle or quarterdeck. In order to maintain four planks to the butt, each subsequent run of planks needs to be set at 20% of the length of the adjoining plank. Note in **Photo 43.2** how the planks are joggled into the margin plank on the deck edge

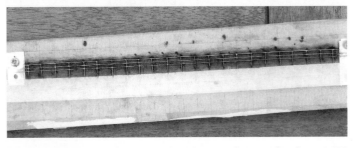

42.1 Jig for forming and soldering three bar stanchions as fitted to a 1:128 KM Blucher.

and how other planks adjoining the margin plank are butt fitted to the waterway.

Planking decks on models

There are a number of timbers that can be used for the planking of model warships, favourites are lime, holly and boxwood. Also there are several method for simulating the caulking. One method that can be used to good effect is to mark one edge of the plank with a black permanent marker before laying into place. Another is to cut the timber into suitable lengths and cut to equal length a section of black paper, apply a thin layer of contact adhesive to the paper. Assemble the planks together so as the ends are all exposed, and place them directly onto the paper and leave to dry. Once the adhesive is set a sharp craft knife can be used to separate each plank along its edge and this has the effect of

43.1 Margin planks are laid around deck fittings, barbettes and to deck edges. USS Wisconsin.

43.2 Joggling to the margin planks. USS Wisconsin.

leaving a fine segment of paper attached to the edge of each plank, **Photo 43.3**.

Stairways - Photo Series 44

There are many different types of stairways depending on the warship. A modern examples is shown here with a Flight 2A "Arleigh Burke" DDG, **Photo 44.1**. Certainly one of the most effective means of reproducing the stairway, particularly at relatively small scales, is to use an etched fret similar to the one shown in **Photo 44.2**, which includes the stringer, treads and hand rails. Equally lengths of stairway can be purchased which are made in resin, white metal or plastic **Photo 44.3**.

Smaller AA gun fits
Bofors 40mm - Photo Series 45

The Bofors 40 mm was fitted in large numbers to many types of warships. The carrier USS Saratoga was fitted with no less than 25 quadruple mountings. An example of the type of mounting used extensively by the USN is seen here on the Museum ship USS Alabama, **Photo 45.1**. The water-cooled quad Mk2 Bofors were on biaxial mountings and in their automatic setting could deliver a rate of fire of 160 rpm.

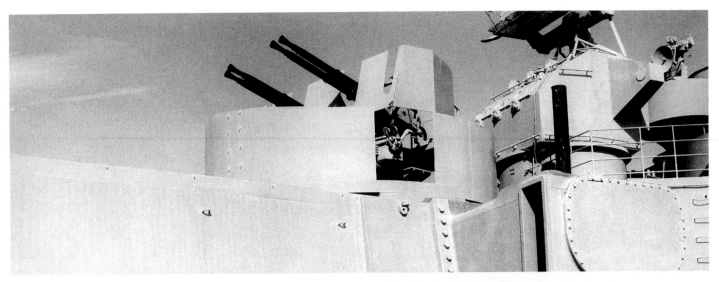

45.1 Quad 40mm AA fit aboard the preserved battleship USS Alabama.

Resin cast 40mm Quads

These resin cast 40mm Mk2s from *John Haynes* are to a scale of 1:96 and are exceptionally well moulded, **Photo 45.2**.

20mm Oerlikon and light gun fits

During WW2, the single 20mm Oerlikon was installed on many allied warships and were all manually operated and free swinging. The rate of fire for this close-in AA weapon was approximately 600 rpm. Like many battleships, North Carolina was extensively fitted as can be seen in **Photo 45.3**.

44.2 Etched fret for treads, stringers and handrails.

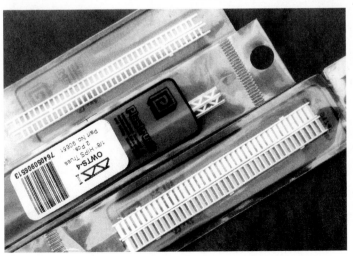

44.3 Plastic stairway and ladders made by Plastruct.

45.2 Superbly cast in resin, Quad 40 by John Haynes.

Cast white metal 20mm

A rather fine example of the 20mm Mk 4 Oerlikon at 1:48 is manufactured by Ted Radestock cast in white metal. Various manufacturers such as *Sirmar*, *John Haynes* and *Floating Dry Dock* have produced the 20mm gun in cast resin and to varying scales, **Photo 45.4**.

Scratch-built MkVIII QF 2 pounder Pom-pom

This magnificent 2 pounder was made by Roy Skeets for a 1:48 Fairmile D and was constructed almost entirely from styrene with many of the actual fittings and moving parts such as the trainers foresight, training hand wheels and pipe work made from brass, **Photo 45.5**. The finished results can be appreciated in **Photo 45.6**.

44.1 Type of stairway fitted to the "Arleigh Burke" class DDG.

45.3 Multiple 20mm Oerlikon mountings as fitted to BB55 North Carolina.

A motorised gun mounting

For effect, gun mountings can be motorised to rotate and elevate the barrels using gearing, micro switches and small drive motors. **Photo 45.7** illustrates this in a 4in gun mounting for a Hunt class DE at 1:48.

45.4 An all-metal 20mm Oerlikon mounting at 1:32.

Above and Below 45.6 2-pounder Pom-pom; a model in its own right.

Cranes - Photo Series 46

Cranes are seen in varying sizes and shapes, generally installed to lift either aircraft or boats or both on carriers, battleships and cruisers. One example is that shown on the battleship North Carolina for lifting the floatplanes from

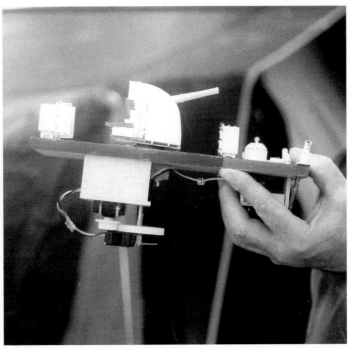

45.7 Using a servo and reduction gearing, a gun can be made to elevate and train.

the water onto the catapults and is basically constructed of tubular steel, **Photos 46.1**. A more modern example is that fitted to the British aviation training ship RFA Argus. A model of this unusual vessel with the crane in place, was built by British modeller Barry Freeman and modelled to 1:96 with the crane on the flight deck abaft of the superstructure to port, **Photo 46.2**.

Reproducing cranes of this type is not difficult. The type shown in **Photo 46.3** fitted to a 1:128 model of KM Blucher has a jib marked and cut from 0.030in styrene sheet and the various pulley wheels cut from etched frets. The jib support arms are 2mm diameter, flattened aluminium tube with the cable guide at the top also from aluminium tube but cut open to feed the cables through.

Torpedo Tubes - Photo Series 47

Torpedo tubes were a common feature of many warships and one of the most effective weapons on destroyers. Following the close of WW2, the torpedo shifted from being an anti-ship weapon to becoming an anti-submarine weapon. However a number of navies retained their torpedo tubes in the anti-ship role, such as this quadruple Soviet 533mm torpedo tube fitted for use with long-range torpedoes **Photo 47.1**.

The basic method used for scratch-building torpedo tubes can be applied to any type. As an example, the tubes shown

46.1 Tubular steel crane as fitted to BB55.

47.1 Torpedo tubes fitted to a Russian Udaloy 1 DDG.

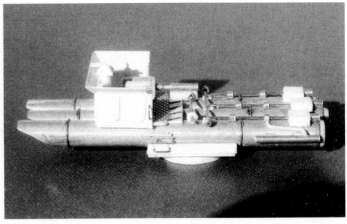

47.2 Aluminium tube forms the torpedo tube, copper wire the piping and styrene the base and platform.

46.2 Heavy lift crane on a 1:96 model of the Air Training Ship RFA Argus.

46.3 Styrene and aluminium tube make up this crane for a 1:128 KM Blucher.

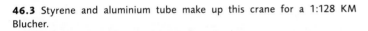

are those fitted to ships of the Kriegsmarine and in this case to a scale of 1:128. Each of the tubes was formed from aluminium, which is easy to work with and most of the other fittings made up from smaller diameter aluminium tube. The loading doors, shielded control platform and base were cut from styrene, Photo 47.2.

Aircraft - Photo Series 48

From the pictures in Chapter 1 showing Ted Parr's realistic USS Nimitz circa 1979, there is little doubt, particularly where carriers are concerned, that the air group finishes the model. This is emphasised here with each aircraft being meticulously researched, **Photo 48.1** (see colour section). Aircraft, like many fittings, are available in kit form or manufactured in resin. Depending on the scale, almost any type of aircraft is available. Also, the air group embarked on this 1:96 model of the RFA Argus carrying Sea King helicopters and Harrier F2As, are all built up from plastic kits, **Photo 48.2**. Again Sea Kings are fitted to a 1:96 LPH HMS Ocean with the forward helicopter made to lift clear of the deck, **Photo 48.3**. As a matter of interest sound effects are incorporated into of the Argus model simulating F2As starting up and working rotors on the Sea Kings.

Modelling helicopters - Photo Series 49

Although many types of aircraft are available, they are not always produced in the required scale. This problem was highlighted when scratch-building the helicopter carrier

48.2 Sea Kings and F2A Harriers on this 1:96 Argus.

48.3 Sea King Mk4s featured aboard this LPH HMS Ocean at 1:96.

Moskva at the unusual scale of 1:125. Not surprisingly, no resin or kit models of KA 25 helicopters existed at 1:125, (**Photo 49.1**) thus it became necessary to scratch-build. Using pattern makers gelutong, a simple drawing and some photos from various publications, a profile was carved to shape using a craft knife (curved blade) and a manicure nail sander, **Photo 49.2**. The flying surfaces and fittings such as doors, rotors, intakes were cut from 0.020in styrene sheet. The landing gear was cut to size from 0.031in brass and bent to conform to the drawing and checked against the pictures of the KA 25. The adhesive of choice was cyanoacrylate.

49.1 Soviet ASW helicopter KA-25 Hormone embarked on Moskva.

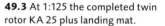

49.2 Carved from the pattern makers timber jellutong. Styrene for the flight surfaces, brass wire for the undercarriage.

49.3 At 1:125 the completed twin rotor KA 25 plus landing mat.

Although not perfect the results were quite satisfying, **Photo 49.3**.

Before resin and plastic kits became available all hobby small-scale model aircraft were built this way. Using this method any type of aircraft can be made to any scale.

Radars - Photo Series 50

Radar arrays fitted to warships have changed significantly over the years with many new warships having fixed, phased array systems like those fitted to the "Arleigh Burke" class of

50.1 The SPY-1 Aegis radar panel as fitted to the USS Ross DDG 71.

50.2 Type 1022 air search radar as fitted to the Type 42 DDG HMS Manchester D95.

50.3 Nato code name Half Plate surface-air search radar as fitted to the Indian DDG Mumbai D62. Note the Russian Influence.

DDGs (**Photo 50.1**) designed to present, like the rest of the ship, a low radar profile. Before "Aegis" warships like CGN 40, the nuclear powered cruiser Mississippi was fitted with the SPS40 B air search mounted on the mainmast. In contrast, there are many warships that retain prominent arrays. For example, the Type 42 HMS Manchester is currently fitted with the Type 1022, a combined surveillance and target identification radar, **Photo 50.2**. The Indian "Delhi" class DDG Mumbai is equipped with the Bharat early warning radar and the Half Plate surface search radar, **Photo 50.3**. Interestingly, these two radars are of Indian/Russian origin, reflecting the co-operation that exists between these two countries on naval matters and are still catalogued using NATO nomenclature, to some degree highlighting the radar appearance. This becomes evident in the radar arrays fitted to the aviation cruiser Moskva.

There are a number of given shapes with the reflectors of naval radars taking on a flat mattress form of wire mesh, parabolic dish type and cheese shapes (see Chapter 1). Thus whatever the shape, it can be made.

Making a radar array - Photo Series 51

For the 1:125 Moskva, these arrays were fabricated using wire mesh and brass wire, **Photo 51.1**. Soldering radar arrays can be a problem particularly as the heat transferred from one part to another unchecked can de-solder earlier joints. To avoid this a heat sink is used. However, these arrays are quite fragile and require a more delicate approach. The answer is the humble paper clip - simple, light and very effective, **Photo 51.2**. Each panel of wire mesh is tied with very fine copper wire to the brass wire framework and to each other, **Photo 51.3**. The Headlight radar presented a different problem and as the reflector was dished

Aluminium car body reinforcing mesh provided the ideal material. This was moulded to shape using an appropriately sized hollow plastic top. The mesh was thumbed into the plastic top and the shape formed, **Photo 51.4**. This was then cut to size and a back plate of styrene wired to the dish, **Photo 51.5**.

Missile launchers - Photo Series 52

Chapter 1 touched on the development of the ship borne missiles and their launchers from the early post war years through to the present day. The missile is now an integral part of a warships anti-ship, anti-submarine and anti-aircraft defence system. Like the big gun, missile launchers come in all shapes and sizes depending on their function. Those shown here are primarily for air defence and use a system of loading and launching that is either (VLS seen on the Type 23 frigate HMS Richmond, (**Photo 52.1**) or using a twin or single arm launcher. Here the missile is either loaded onto the launcher horizontally from loading doors immediately to the rear of the launcher as fitted to the CGN USS Long Beach, **Photo 52.2**, or vertically from doors sited

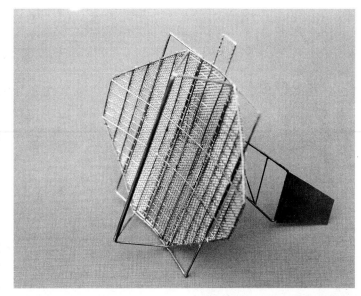

51.1 Above Scratch built Nato code Top Sail air search radar for Moskva.

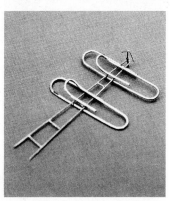

51.2 Right The simple expedient of a paperclip make for an effective heat shunt when soldering.

51.3 Below Nato code Head Net C radar made using a combination of wire mesh and brass wire.

on the base of the launcher where missiles are stored on a carousel system below decks. Examples of the latter are the single arm Mk13 Mod 4 version fitted to the "Perry" class of FFGs **Photo 52.3**.

There are two distinct types: the long-range missile, which requires some form of booster and the more agile close-range missile. For example the post war 953cm Talos was a long-range missile and used a solid fuel rocket with a ramjet sustainer motor. A further example is the Sea Dart missile and launcher presently used by the RN on the type 42 destroyers. The missile like Talos combines a solid propellant

51.4 Aluminium wire, ideal material to form dished radar arrays.

51.5 Part of the twin "Head Light" director array for Moskva.

rocket with a ramjet and as such has a range of over 42nm.

Modelling a missile launcher

Fittings such as missile launchers are available from manufactures either in mini-kit form or fully moulded in resin and generally made to accompany one of the semi kits available within the manufacturers range Naturally manufacturers of resin fittings do not make every type and scale possible therefore it rests with the modeller to make fittings such as the missile launcher.

The Soviet aviation cruiser Moskva is one such example where launchers needed to be made from scratch to a scale of 1:125. Thankfully some pictures were available, as was a reasonable modeller's drawing, **Photo 52.4**. The same method can be used to make any single or twin arm launcher regardless of type. The plinth that supports the arms and is mounted to the deck is made of either styrene tube as in the SUW-N-1 launcher forward or the SAN-1 launcher featured in the centre of the photo. A tapering mount is formed by using either gelutong timber or cutting the base and top of the pillar then connecting these up at the correct height and using Bondaglass or a fine filler to fill in between. Once the filler has set this can be sanded down to give a true and smooth surface. The arms are made from gelutong although

52.1 VLS on the British FFG HMS Richmond.

52.2 Terrier missile, twin arm launcher on CGN USS Long Beach. Note the loading doors abaft of the launcher.

52.3 Mk 13 Mod 4 single arm launcher.

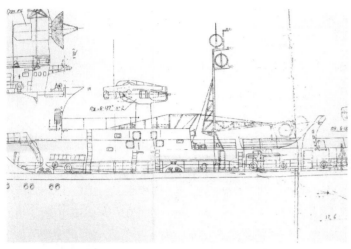

52.4 Part of the drawing showing the SAN-3 missile launcher.

52.5 SAN-3 launcher with SUW-NI missile launcher forward

balsa will suffice. The timber is cut to the shape shown on the drawing and covered with 0.010in styrene sheet. Equally the support part for the launcher arms can be made using the same method. To support the arms, a length of brass rod is passed through pre-drilled holes from arm to arm, **Photo 52.5**. The fully assembled and painted launchers can be seen in **Photo 52.6**. Note the two horseshoe ASW RBU 6000 rocket launchers forward of the SUW-N-1 launcher.

General fittings - Photo Series 53

Naturally there are a huge number of small fixtures and fittings on warships of any period and inevitably fittings as such change but their function often remains the same. A number of fittings that are frequently seen on warships are shown.

Moving anchor cables

All warships are fitted with anchor cables and a method of hauling and lowering the anchor. **Photo 53.1** shows a windlass usually fitted to smaller warships such as this "Sandown" class Mine Hunter. The cable (anchor chain) is made temporarily secure by fittings that are termed Blake Slip Stoppers and

53.1 Windlass as fitted to a RN Sandown class MCMV mine countermeasures vessel

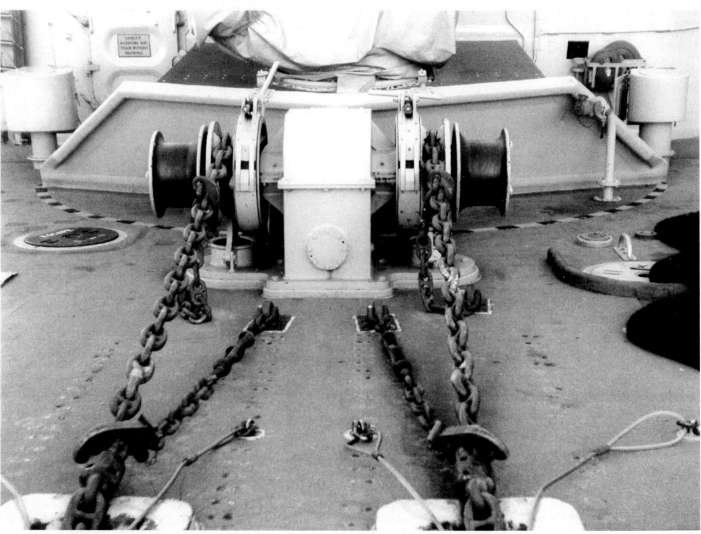

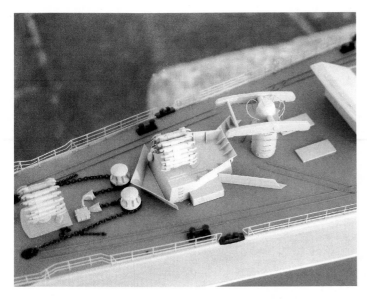

52.6 Completed launchers on Moskva.

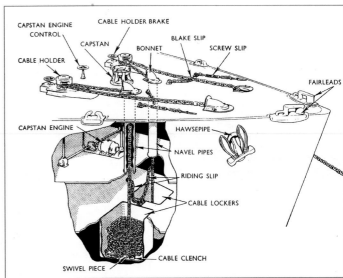

Fig 53.1 Typical forecastle arrangement for operating the anchors.

Screw Stoppers. The Blake slips are fitted with a clip holding the cable at one end and a shackle and eye plate fitted to the deck. The screw stopper is similar to a Blake slip but is fitted with a bottle screw for the purpose of securing the anchor close into the hawse pipe.

Larger warships are usually fitted with "cable holders" with the cable drawn up or lowered through the navel pipes into the chain or cable lockers, **Fig 53.1**. To work the cable stops and snugs are fitted to the lower part of the cable holder and are shaped to key into the links of the chain. Adjacent to the holder is the brake wheel, which is used in conjunction with the cable holder when raising or lowering the anchor, **Photo 53.2**.

53.5 large cordage reel as fitted to USS Alabama BB 60.

53.2 Cable holder with the bonnet covering the opening to the NAVEL pipe

53.3 Panama Bows rope guide.

53.4 Assortment of various sized ventilators on the Heavy cruiser HMS Belfast. *(Photo Tony Ansell)*

Rope guides mooring rings

Mooring rings are a section of cast steel where cordage is rove through for the purpose of securing the ship to a berth. One of the most common is called a Panama bow, **Photo 53.3.**

Ventilators

Deck ventilators are seen in a variety of shapes and sizes and are used to vent the spaces below. There are many other types which are fitted to deck housings and are for ventilation of engine spaces and air filtration systems seen here on HMS Belfast, **Photo 53.4.**

Cordage Reels

Cordage reels come in a variety of sizes and are used for the stowage of rope. Some are fitted to the sides of deck housings. There are much larger reels generally for wire rope secured to the deck. This example is from the battleship USS Alabama BB 60, **Photo 53.5.** In fact in the same picture there are a number of recognisable fittings that have been discussed in this chapter.

Fire fighting equipment

Fire fighting equipment is often overlooked in magazines and books dealing with fittings on naval vessel but is one

53.7 How ladders are secured to the superstructure.

53.9 Clip Type "B" hatch with emergency escape hatch.

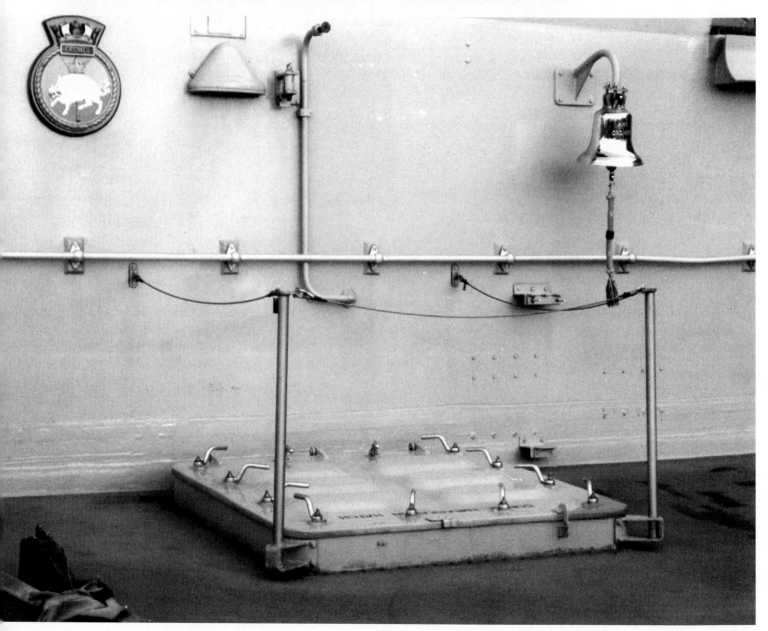

53.8 below Clip Type "A" hatch on RN ships.

53.10 BALDT type stockless anchor as fitted to the USS Wisconsin BB64.

Fig 53.2 AC 14 high holding stockless anchor.

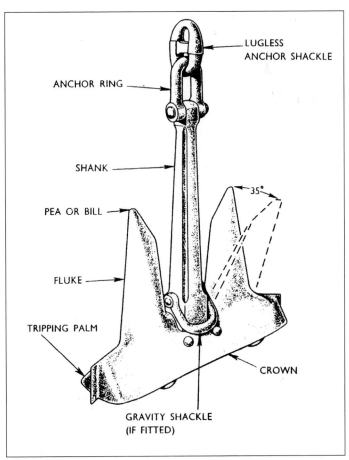

of the most vital features. Although the needs remain the same regardless of navy, the fitting arrangement for fire fighting equipment can differ. **Photo 53.6** (see colour section) illustrates the arrangement on an "Arleigh Burke" class DDG and the method used for stowage of the hose, which is common to all modern USN warships.

Ladders

Ladders abound on any warship. Those fitted to masts, deck housings and superstructures are fitted in much the same way, generally with a support for the ladder frame being welded to the side of the plating and the ladder bolted to the supports, **Photo 53.7**.

Watertight hatches

Watertight hatches come in all shapes and sizes but there are two basic methods of opening a hatch as defined in the RN, clip type "B" **Photo 53.9** or clip type "A", **Photo**

53.8the latterdesigned so as it can be released from below. A combination of the two has a small escape manhole in the centre of the hatch, **Photo 53.9**.

Anchors

Anchors are present in a variety of sizes and shapes. Generally their purpose is the same - to hold the ship in position. The anchor is designed in such away that as it lies flat along the sea bottom, the strain on the cable pulls it along until the tipping palm tilts the flukes and they dig in; **Fig 53.2** illustrates an AC14 high-holding stockless anchor used by RN warships. **Photo 53.10** shows a Baldt type stockless anchor as fitted to the USS Wisconsin BB64.

Chapter Nine

Painting and camouflage

It is believed in some quarters that paint used on models will cover surface defects or that the more coats the better the finish. These are just a two of the myths that have been believed at one time or another and will be explored more fully in this chapter. Painting a model is an acquired skill, but weathering is an art form. One of the most inspiring examples of weathering that I have seen was produced by a Belgian modeller which will be discussed later in this chapter.

Questions are regularly asked as to how the paintwork on warship models should be best tackled in relation to both the selection of the type of paint, and the more complex issues surrounding the appropriate camouflage scheme for a particular ship.

Further questions asked are:

a) What is the best method of application, either brush or spray or a combination of both?
b) How best to prepare a given surface to receive paint?
c) What type of primer is best used for styrene?

These and more related questions will be discussed later in this chapter.

It is often maintained that no ship is pristine when it goes down the ways or as it leaves the fitting-out basin for the first time. To some extent this is true but when a ship is being commissioned for the first time, then the paintwork is to the highest standard with perhaps the exception of ships commissioned in wartime. Thus, at some point in a life of a warship, the paintwork can be considered to be close to a pristine finish.

Interestingly there are many misconceptions that have built up regarding the whole aspect of camouflage. Before

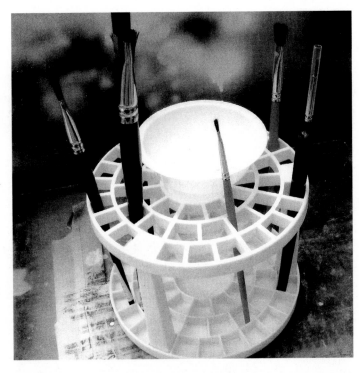

54.1 A collection of varying size, good quality sable brushes.

exploring the subject of camouflage further, there are some basic requirements that need to be considered.

Preparation and to brush or not to brush - Photo Series 54

The first decision to be made is the means by which paint is applied; either brush or spray. Both can give excellent results but the final outcome depends on the quality of preparation and the type of brush or airbrush used.

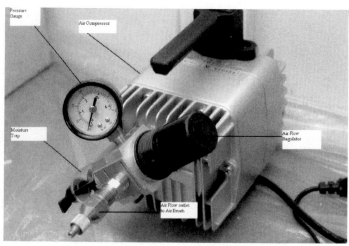

55.1 Above Good quality air compressor with moisture trap.

54.2 Left Simple but effective means of spraying large areas.

54.3 Below With adjustable head, a more effective means of airbrushing.

56.1 Bottom Scratch built Rurik hull having received a basic primer coat.

57.1 Fine filling agents can be used even on styrene.

57.2 Deckhouse fittings in place ready to receive a primer coat.

57.3 Fine details should not be hidden by too many coats of paint.

57.4 An over deck which can be painted and fitted later.

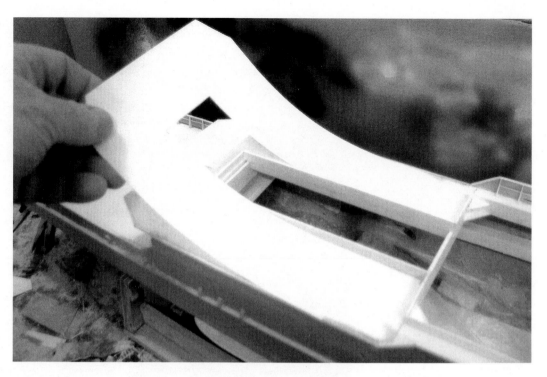

The quality of the tools used is very important. A good quality sable brush may appear expensive but is a valuable purchase that should reward the user with a high standard of paint finish. A fair selection of brush head sizes and shapes is also a wise investment. A wide flat head suitable for painting large areas will be of little use for painting intricate parts of a gun breech, **Photo 54.1**.

Equally a basic single-action airbrush can be bought which will be fine if the requirement is to blanket cover a hull or superstructure (**Photo 54.2**) but a more sophisticated dual-action model will be needed for fine detail work. Simple, inexpensive single-action airbrushes can be a valuable tool for providing an introduction into the art of air brushing and will allow the user to feel confident enough to progress to a more expensive type, **Photo 54.3**.

Air canisters and compressors - Photo Series 55

The airbrush requires a propellant of compressed air delivered from either a canister of air or from a compressor. Once again the cost element is a factor affecting choice. In the long term, the canister of air is almost certainly the most expensive option even if it appears to be the reverse initially. The volume of spray work expected to be embarked upon is a factor that needs to be considered for, in the long term, a compressor is bound to be the cheaper solution.

Many working models will be in the medium to large size range thus the cost to spray will be high if the source was to be canisters of air alone. Whilst the purchase of an air compressor such as the one illustrated would initially be high, this would be offset over a period of time as such a unit would be available for many models. In **Photo 55.1** various pointers denote parts of the typical airbrush compressor.

Preparation for painting
Applying fillers to plank on frame hull -
Photo Series 56

Fillers can be any one of a number of proprietary brands for example P38. Target only those areas that need to be filled as blanket covering just makes unnecessary work. Generally a well-planked, well-prepared hull will require only a fraction of the filling paste required by a less well-prepared hull. When set, the fillers can be gently rubbed down with a medium fine wet and dry, remembering to bear in mind health and safety considerations. Don't rub down fillers in a confined space and always wear some form of protective mask.

Rubbing down and adding filler may need to be repeated more than once depending on how well the hull has been prepared. Eventually a point will be reached when the surface of the hull has become completely uniform. The hull can remain unpainted at this point until further constructional work is undertaken but a covering of primer will help in identifying any further parts of the hull that may require filling. The primer of choice is "High Build", an acrylic based product that will fill any minor scratches or surface imperfections. This is not a substitute for tardy preparation. The results of applying the primer can be seen in, **Photo 56.1**. Incidentally any openings in the hull such as portholes, hawse pipes and cooling intakes can be made at any time after treatment with fillers.

The hull needs to be held firmly during subsequent stages of building by bolting to a portable baseboard. The holes made can be easily filled when the hull is ready for its final coat of paint.

Preparation of GRP and styrene - Photo Series 57

With a growing number of semi-kits now available, the hull and perhaps a deck and even part of the superstructure will be moulded in GRP. These will need to be thoroughly cleaned with a liquid detergent in order to remove any remaining traces of release agent used in the moulding process and the surface gently rubbed down with a fine wet and dry.

Styrene is a versatile material and devoid of grain and like GRP should be cleaned with liquid detergent that helps reduce static, as this can have a detrimental effect on the adhesion of the paint.

Modern filling agents such as Plasto or Green Fillers have an exceptionally fine texture and as such make for a good filling agent for styrene. Both bond well to the surface at very fine levels of thickness, even down to 0.030in. The results and an example are illustrated on the 1:96 model of HMS Mersey, **Photo 57.1**. As mentioned in Chapter 6, deckhouse fittings such as WT doors, ladders and rails can be set in place to be

59.2 With the anti foul completed the same method as in Photo 59.1 can be employed for the boot topping.

58.1 Low tack masking tape is ideal for masking between colours.

59.3 Boot topping neat and clean.

painted with the superstructure or any other deck housings, **Photo 57.2** and **57.3**.

Although adding a layer to the existing deck, the removable 0.010in styrene deck surface, on the model of HMS Mersey, is a useful way of highlighting that fine divide between bulwark, deck edge and deck surface without the need for masking off and can be painted the correct pale blue of the non-slip surface and added later, **Photo 57.4**.

Painting the hull and superstructure

Once the preparation is completed the hull and superstructure can be spray or brush painted. Colour schemes largely depend

59.1 Simple expedient of set square and pencil for marking the correct line of the anti foul.

on a time period and this will be discussed further in this chapter.

It is good practice to mix the full quantity of each of the colours that will be required to complete the model before commencing, to avoid problems of shade consistency from batch to batch.

Choice of paint

For those involved in model ship building either static or larger scale working models, there are two types of paints in general use, acrylic and enamel. Cellulose based paints are seldom used by the scale ship modeller and tend to be the preserve of those involved in aeromodelling. The range of colours and shades available in enamels and acrylics is quite extensive, particularly from specialist suppliers (see Appendix 3). Enamels are usually oil based whilst acrylics are water based and the thinning agents are different; white spirit for enamels and isopropanol for acrylics.

In order to get paints to flow more effectively and increase coverage they will need to be thinned. When using enamel paints from a brush some modellers prefer (and get better results) to use paint fresh from the tin with no added thinners. Others prefer to add thinners by percentage. There is no absolute on this subject. However when using an airbrush it becomes essential to thin down any type of paint. From personal experience 50% thinners to 50% paint by volume is

60.1 Fine detail can also be added after the initial primer coat.

61.2 A wooden raft with fittings attached ready for painting.

a benchmark figure. Drying times also differ. Enamels usually require at least 6 hours to be thoroughly dry whilst acrylics take approximately 2hours.

Cleaning down
The agents for cleaning brushes and spray equipment are dependent on the type of paint. Enamels are best cleansed with white spirit, whilst water is best for acrylics.

61.1 Fittings on a revolving table in preparation for painting.

It can't be stressed enough the value of a good cleaning regime, as brushes and air brushes are only as good as the last job. For air brushes or other spraying equipment dismantle the unit and, depending on the paint used, wash down each component part until satisfied that all traces of paint have been removed. Only then can a spray gun or airbrush be considered clean and ready for the next job.

Masking - Photo Series 58
When considering masking off one surface from another the choice of masking tape can be quite critical. Standard masking tape found at most household or car accessory outlets has too much adhesive power, enough in fact to remove a relatively newly painted surface. As an alternative there is what is known as low tack tape, which has sufficient strength to adhere to a freshly painted surface, and when removed leaves a clean sharp edge with no creep. But unlike conventional masking tape, low tack allows the original surface to remain unmarked, **Photo58.1**.

Anti-fouling and boot toping
Anti fouling for full size ships is a type of paint that is formulated to be resistant to marine growth and as such is used on the underside of hulls. The boot topping, which is a narrow band of paint, usually between the light and deep water lines, is formulated to withstand the constant wetting and drying which occurs in service. The colour or shade can vary depending on the particular navy and the time period when the ship was built.

Method of application to models - Photo Series 59
My favoured method for marking the level of the anti-fouling is to have the hull exactly upright on a flat surface. Using a set square, temporally fit a 2H pencil to the square and allow sufficient overhang to accommodate any undercut in the bow and at a position that corresponds with the level of the anti–fouling. This level is generally shown on GA drawings or those

supplied with the hull or kit. Run the marking square along the length of the hull on each side, **Photo 59.1**. Once the level is marked, low tack tape can be gently thumbed into place. If an airbrush is to be used, the exposed upper half of the hull should be completely covered over. The lower half of the hull is now prepared and ready to be painted. Once dry the tape can be removed and the procedure repeated for the boot topping, **Photo 59.2**. The final results should be a clean and crisp line regardless of depth, **Photo 59.3**. Avoid the temptation to use vinyl tape for the boot topping as this can easily peel.

Superstructures - Photo Series 60

Superstructure and deck housings are best removed from the hull and sprayed separately. A primer coat, usually a base

62.1 Dazzle camouflage as applied to vessels in WW1. *(Photo Merseyside Maritime Museum)*

grey (or even matt white) is first applied.

If the base surface is well prepared then a single coat is far more desirable than multiple coats. If there are fittings such as ladders, scuttles, eye brows, eye plates, piping, or rails fitted to any of the deck housings, then multiple coats of paint have the effect of interfering with and blurring the detail, whilst keeping paint to the minimum will highlight the detail. **Photo 60.1** illustrates this point where the main superstructure on Moskva was given a coat of primer and the more detailed fittings, such as ladders rails and watertight doors added later.

Painting fittings - Photo Series 61

It should be a fundamental principle that fittings made or bought in, need to be well prepared to accept a brush or spray paint finish. In fact those made from scratch are probably easier to prepare than those from resin or white metal that may require flash removing.

Regardless of application painting fittings can pose problems depending on type and size. I have made use of a number of methods that allow for a little flexibility of application. Take for example that shown in **Photo 61.1**, which uses a revolving table with the fittings distributed on the adhesive side of ordinary masking tape. A number of the larger fittings can be secured in place with double side adhesive tape on lengths of timber, with others fittings such as davits and vents, placed in pre-drilled holes. A notable advantage of this method is that the fittings can be lifted and moved around in any direction whilst painting, **Photo 61.2**.

Spray booth

The spray booth can be very useful when air brushing indoors. The spray booth works well although it is limited in capacity to fittings and small superstructures. Here fittings are placed on a revolving table, as the direction of the spray remains constant. For painting a hull, the best option is to wait for favourable conditions and spray in the open.

Camouflage for warship models

Next to weathering, camouflage is probably one of the more misunderstood aspects of warship modelling. There are a number of excellent publications that discuss in detail many of the aspects of camouflage at sea. Official codes are available and are well documented in publications such as "Naval Camouflage 1914 - 1945" by David Williams, or Peter Hodges earlier publication "Royal Navy Warship Camouflage". Both go into great detail deriving much of their information from official sources.

However for the modeller extrapolating this information it is very subjective as photos of the period, either black and white or colour, can be misleading because there is always the element of light distortion and more importantly fading of negatives or prints. Some do give a true reading and the picture you see is exactly what the camera sees. But here again what the human eye sees may not be what the camera sees.

What is official is also open to debate as batches of paint stored aboard ships were often applied under wartime conditions thus shades were not always matched.

63.2 Western Approaches Green effectively applied by Ted Parr to his fine
1:48 model of HMS Starling.

63.3 A good representation by Peter Dicker of the Individual Pattern Scheme
applied to HMS Valiant.

Purpose of camouflage - Photo Series 62

The purpose of camouflage is to conceal and deceive. It was during WW1 that a truly scientific approach was taken with the principle leader in the UK being Norman Wilkinson a marine artist, and in the USA Lloyd Ancile Jones a scientist for the Eastman Kodak research laboratories.

Norman Wilkinson proposed the concept of "dazzle" painting with deception as its prime purpose, particularly that relating to the true course of the vessel. It is interesting to note that bright, heavily contrasting colours in geometric patterns were arranged differently on either side of the ship. The principle is well illustrated in this model of the SS Spennymore using a design by Norman Wilkinson and now a feature at the Mersey Maritime Museum, Liverpool, UK, **Photo 62.1**.

Examples of camouflage schemes - Photo Series 63

From the beginning of WW2 the Admiralty issued instructions on camouflage in the form of Confidential Admiralty Fleet orders (CAFOs) and Admiralty Fleet Orders (AFOs). For example CAFO 679 relates to the Western Approaches Scheme conceived unofficially by the artist Peter Scott and unlike the previous dazzle patterns used concealment as its core principle. For this scheme, white became the base colour with the rest of the hull and superstructure incorporating light blue and light green; officially given the code WAB and WAG respectively. An illustration of how this scheme may have appeared, as applied to a 1:48 model of the Type 2 "Hunt"

65.1 LST-1074 looking very weathered. *(Photo Nobie Smith)*

class destroyer HMS Ledbury by Peter Dicker, **Photo 63.1** (see colour section).

The Admiralty used a system of prefixes denoting colours for example MS-1 would be grey black whilst 507A is very dark grey. A further example gives an impression at least in model form, of the effectiveness of these schemes in certain light and water conditions. **Photo 63.2**, a 1:48 "Black Swan" class escort sloop HMS Starling by Ted Parr, indicates clearly how the light green WAG seems to merge with the reflectivity of the water. This of course cannot be taken as a direct comparison with the original but nonetheless an interesting comparison can be drawn. As a point of interest the model of Starling used Humbrol 156 (satin dark camouflage grey), 64 (matt light grey) and a blend of sea green with matt light grey.

Although the four official camouflage schemes were used on smaller warships such as destroyers and sloops, larger warships such as cruisers, carriers and battleships were often singled out for special treatment under "Individual Patterns". Although using the basic schemes then in use these were adapted to suit a particular ship. A good example of this is the scheme applied to HMS Valiant seen here on a 1:128 model by Peter Dicker, **Photo 63.3**.

Camouflage on ships of the USN - Photo Series 64

Camouflage used on USN ships was as varied and complex as that applied to RN warships and any in-depth appraisal is out of the scope of this publication. There are publications wholly devoted to the subject and one such book, with modellers firmly in mind, is "USN Warship Camouflage 1939-1945" by Chris Ellis and is highly recommended.

The implementation and development of camouflage for

64.1 Measure 22 on the Fletcher class DD USS Kidd.

64.3 Ron Horribin's North Carolina in Measure 32/18D.

warships in the USN was the overall responsibility of the Bureau of Ships, from the introduction of Measure 1 (which was in fact dark grey overall) through to Measure 33. In all there were 25 primary camouflage "measures" which did not, as would be implied, follow a direct numerical order. Measure 33, being what has been described as the ultimate refinement for anti-submarine camouflage in low visibility conditions in both the northern latitudes of the Pacific and Atlantic.

Measure 22 was one of the best known, as it was designed for ships operating in the South and West pacific and used dark navy blue part way up the hull but parallel with the boot topping for the length of the hull. Above this line and including the superstructure, the vessel was painted in haze grey and the effect was for the ship to blend in with both sea and sky. **Photo 64.1** shows Measure 22 on the "Fletcher" class destroyer USS Kid now a museum ship at Baton Rouge, Louisiana.

A fine example of camouflage and the skill of the modeller, is well illustrated in **Photos 64.2** (see colour section) of the heavy cruiser CL49 USS St Louis at 1:192, scratch built by US modeller Don Pruel and dressed overall in measure 32/2. It is interesting to note, particularly on the model of the St Louis, the stark differences in the shape and shading on each side of the ship with those of the USS Baltimore with its bold irregular splinter patterns reminiscent of those earlier WW1

67.1 Norwegian low radar visible Air Cushion Guided Missile Patrol Boat.

designs. The use of camouflage is again well demonstrated on this 1:96 working scale model of the North Carolina using the measure 32/18D, **Photo 64.3**.

Weathering - Photo Series 65
Camouflage is an acquired skill; weathering is an art form. Warship paint work if neglected, either by the demands of war or the rigours being at sea, can produce effects that will alter the intended appearance of the paint finishes to a considerable extent. To translate this into model form and give an authentic feel to the ship, is a task that requires great care as the border line between what looks right and what is garish is very narrow indeed. Take for example **Photo 65.1** of the LST 1074. It is hard to decide whether the ship was camouflaged and the painted work then eroded, or whether there was only ever a single colour used but the effect actually tells a story. This is no newcomer to battle or the sea and has seen much action. By contrast the vintage "Essex" class carrier USS Wasp CVS 18, as in 1971, has rust marks and streaks along the hull, **Photo 65.2** (see colour section).

Examples of convincing weathering - Photo Series 66
The following pictures are certainly among the most outstanding examples of weathering on model warships. This working model of the Belgian "Flower" class corvette Godetia (ex-HMS Dart) at 1:48, not only shows the rust but also the

effect of a faded Western Approaches camouflage scheme. Rust does develop along certain tracks like wash ports from points where fittings are mounted around the deck edges and on the upper rails.

Equally, exposed steel deck although constantly walked on will show rust and note the effective way rust has been blended along the water line, **Photo 66.1** (see colour section).

Modern and future camouflage - Photo Series 67
Modern camouflage, whilst relying more and more on radar reflective surfaces and methods of reducing IR emissions for concealment, still relies on scientifically prepared paints to achieve visual concealment but, no ship in the visual band can be made to be invisible. Yet efforts are always being made to achieve a degree of visual concealment that would be an improvement on camouflage schemes of the past. The Norwegian Navy in a fairly radical shift, have with this new design combined the advantages of air cushion, multi hull form, water jet propulsion with an advanced radar reflective shape. Add to these, new constructional materials and a painted camouflage scheme to suit the waters close to Norway and far northern latitude. The result is the Skjold, a warship combining the best features of radar concealment with the latest in visual camouflage technology, **Photos 67.1**.

Chapter Ten

Preparation and operation

Transport and storage of models - Photo Series 68

Once the paintwork has been completed, there remains one last job before a model gets its first outing. Given all the effort lavished on a new model, then that last job is some form of case for storage and transport, regardless of whether the model is a working or non-working. The box shown in **Photo 68.1** is made up of 4mm ply with 1in square battens giving internal support. The front can be constructed from ply or acrylic sheet that can slide out on grooves, and the box then doubles as a showcase. The alternative is a simple case using

eyelets with screws to secure the front cover. To further protect the fragile contents, the inside between the battens can be filled by polystyrene sheet. Last but not least are carrying handles, which should be bolted to the top of the box, one in the middle and two at either end for maximum strength. If help is available the box and contents can be moved quite easily. Finally a coat of yacht varnish can be applied to the exterior, this is both durable and long lasting regardless of the weather.

Depending on the size of the model, transport can present problems. Perhaps a little obvious, but a simple rule of thumb is to make certain that when considering a new model, the transport available is adequate and the model can be accommodated safely. The second advantage of a case is in storage. To my mind workshops are not good storage spaces for finished models but as

68.1 A case offers good protection from accidental damage during transit and storage.

69.2 A fully ballasted Russian Aviation cruiser Moskva.

often happens that is the only space available. Thus a case becomes invaluable in minimising the possibility of accidental damage. Keeping the model enclosed and away from dust reduces the potential for further damage, as the simple procedure of cleaning can become a hazard in itself.

Footnote to choice of subject - Photo Series 69
Working models, unlike their static counterparts have to be a compromise between the desire for fine detail, the need to handle the model frequently and access into the interior of the

hull. A good example of this is in the building of warships of a period where significant amounts of rigging were still in use, and is illustrated well in this 1:96 armoured cruiser HMS Kent, Photo 69.1 (see colour section). Such a model would grace any

70.1 A traditional unballasted launch even for a model.

70.3 Ballasting out a 1:96 North Carolina.

ballasting and trimming was completed at a very early stage of the build, **Photo 69.2**.

Ballasting and trim - Photo Series 70

It is helpful if the internal installation and ballasting trials are carried out prior to the deck being fitted into place. However this is not always possible and ballasting may have to remain one of the last jobs to be undertaken before a model can be launched successfully.

Even then, a sense of the theatrical may be enough to persuade some modellers to launch their models in a more traditional way. This 1:96 model of the battleship Tirpitz is one such example, **Photo 70.1**. A further two models built by Task Force 72 members taking to the water for the first time USS Tarawa LHA1 at 1:72 scale and a 1:72 DDG 81 USS Winston Churchill. Models of this size require significant levels of ballast. **Photo 70.2**.

It is basic logic that the bigger the model, the more ballast will be needed to make the model rest on its waterline. Although that does not always imply a model is in the best trim position or will sail correctly; the two conditions are not the same.

In **Photo 70.3**, Ron Horabin is, with some assistance, ballasting his model of the North Carolina using two Panasonic 12v, 7Ah lead-acid batteries placed amidships. Complementing this ballast is 23 pounds of flat lead just forward of the same position and a trim weight of 5 pounds beneath the turret. Note also that to help with lifting the hull the barbettes can be removed. Once loaded, the superstructure is put in place and the model is ready to run. Although the hull is made of balsa and comfortable to lift even for one person, the entire model minus ballast weighs in at around 40 pounds giving an all up weight of 78 pounds.

Water ballast - Photo Series 71

As an alternative to lead, water can be used, eliminating much of the dead weight that needs to be transported with the model. Water tanks can be made using styrene, acrylic, Perspex, metal, even timber. **Photo 71.1 & 71.2** show a model of the Victorian turret ship Devastation taking on water. This particular model

71.2 Devastation ballasted and ready to get underway

static exhibition as a glass case exhibit yet compromises have had to be made to enable parts of the superstructure to be lifted clear of the deck.

The same is true for other types of warships for example, the carrier where there is often a large expanse of open deck and with a working model, compromise is inevitable. This is evident on Ted Parr's Nimitz where the centre section can be lifted clear and the joints in the deck are an unwelcome, but inevitable, compromise.

The desire to retain maximum authenticity of appearance, whilst gaining as much access into the hull as possible is in itself is a compromise; this was borne out when building Moskva. In order to have an unbroken deck area the only access into the hull was through the removal of the superstructure. Thus all the

70.2 Ballasting and trimming 1:72 USS Tarawa and the USS Winston S
Churchill. *(Photo Michael Brown)*

71.1 Perspex ballast tanks fitted to a 1:48 model of HMS Devastation.

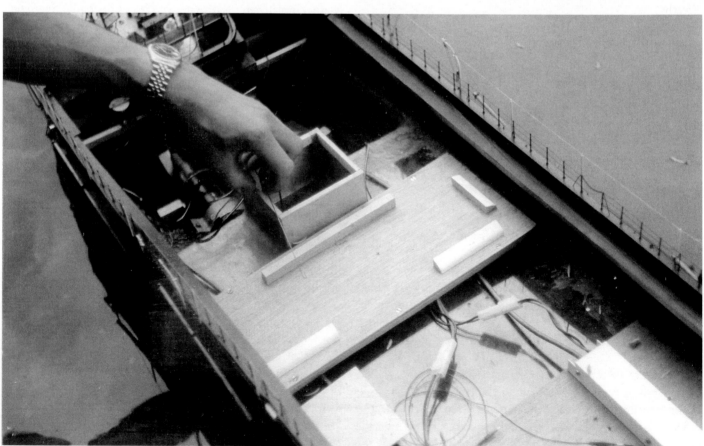

is to a scale of 1:48 therefore quite large and having a significant amount of water to displace.

Draft versus stability

For many years it was accepted by builders of working models that improving stability required an increase in the draft of the hull, especially in warship models with a narrow beam to length ratio. Whilst this method was considered acceptable for working models, it was seen by many true scale modellers at the time as being distinctly un-scale like when out of the water, which of course it was. With the advent of GRP hulls and the shift to using drawings more representative of the full size vessel, the practice of increasing the draft of the hull waned and a more scale approach adopted to the practice of ballasting and trimming.

Trimming a working model - Photo Series 72

Naturally enough, the problems of ballasting and correctly trimming working warship models remained, and it was thought that putting enough weight as low as possible in the hull would solve the problem. Unfortunately this approach does produce what is termed a "stiff" ship. As a ship goes into a turn the natural effect is to heel, this is particularly evident on narrower beam hulls. **Photo 72.1** shows a 1:128 model of the cruiser HMS Manchester turning to port. In a stiff ship the length of time taken for the vessel to change from heeled to upright is quite brief, whilst for a well-trimmed hull this return motion is much slower.

To reduce the prospect of having a stiff ship, ballast for trimming is best placed up the side of the hull at a point below the centre of gravity and above the centre of buoyancy. The purpose of this is to reduce the distance between the Centre of Gravity (C of G or CG) and the metacentric height, **Fig 72.1**. It is worth remembering that the position of the metacentre is directly dependent on the moment of inertia of the water plane. If this is increased the metacentre will rise and so increase the initial stability.

Although the model ship is easily inclined, it returns to the upright position slowly with an easy motion, following that of a full-size ship. Whilst **Photo 72.2** highlights the positioning of the ballast using lengths of sheet lead. These are fitted underneath the shafts following the shape of the bilge and up the side of the hull, further trimming pieces are placed forward. The result is a well-trimmed model with realistic performance, **Photo 72.3** (see colour section).

Moving models to water - Photo Series 73

Sailing waters for model ships vary considerably with some having easy access and others requiring some effort to get the model into the water. Moving working model warships from the bank side to water has the potential; if not thought through, to either be the source of some future back problem or result in some damage to the model. With this in mind it is worth looking at several ways that modellers employ to make that transition less of a potential hazard.

One of the most widely used methods is a sling used when lifting a sizeable 1:128 HMS Valiant, **Photo 73.1**. The principle works regardless of size, with a crane and sling lifting a 2 ton, 28ft carrier HMS Invincible owned by Duncan Cameron, **Photo 73.2**.

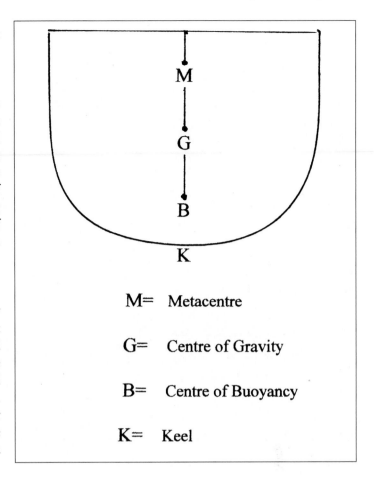

M= Metacentre

G= Centre of Gravity

B= Centre of Buoyancy

K= Keel

Fig 72.1 Ballast is better placed in a position below the centre of gravity but above the centre of buoyancy.

EVENTS AND SHOWS

On the water events world wide - Photo Series 74)

Interest in model warships (static or working) is worldwide and events can vary from an enthusiasts gathering to a full-blown competitive event. A good example of this is the national gathering of Task Force 72 in Australia, where all the models are put on general display on the water and then form a sail past. Just about every form of model is represented and not just ships of the RAN but a full international Fleet Review. Quite an achievement considering that many of those attending events like this have to travel great distances to take part. One such event takes place at Wentworth falls in the Blue Hills near Sydney where all the models are to a constant 1:72, **Photo 74.1**.

In the UK there have been numerous events for warship modellers where such models have been well represented. **Photo 74.2** shows the pre-dreadnought battleship HMS Queen at a maritime model show held appropriately in the grounds of the National Maritime Museum. Certainly one of the oldest and best attended is the Potteries' Navy Day. A competitive event held annually in August involving static exhibits, navigation, working features demonstrations and even formation sailing. **Photo 74.3** gives some flavour of this event.

Statically displayed warship models - Photo Series 75

Events such as Dortmund model show, certainly Europe's biggest, positively encourages specialist displays such as this group of

72.1 Although this 1:128 model of the cruiser HMS Manchester heels, the return is easy and more authentic.

72.2 Flat strip lead is situated up the side of the hull to act as trim ballast.

German modellers dedicated to US Carriers. Even the entrance to this display has the feel of being inside the hanger of a carrier **Photo 75.1**. A model group under the name of Kaiserliche Marine, build and display warships of the Imperial German Navy and have constructed as part of their display an indoor pool complete with docks, railway system and of course, warships, **Photo 75.2**. The Model Engineer Exhibition held annually in the Greater London area has been setting the standard for statically judged models for over 70 years and as such has earned a reputation for encouraging some of the best builders of warships.

Typical of the very high standard required even for working models is Dave Abbots superb HMS Iveston, a "Ton" class minesweeper and a Gold medal winner at the Model Engineer Exhibition. See Chapter 1.

Working features - Photo Series 76

At the Potteries' Navy Day a 1:72 model of the LPD HMS Fearless with a fully working and independently controlled LCVP was seen. The stern door drops and the after part of the hull is partly flooded by filling chambers on either side of the dock. This permits the LCVP to float out as per the real ship, **Photos 76.1**. Equally ingenious are the electro-mechanical methods employed on this scratch-built model of the carrier HMS Illustrious built

73.1 Using a rope sling - a simple yet effective way of lifting a model from the stand to water.

73.2 A slightly larger sling to lift a 28ft model HMS Invincible but the principle remains the same regardless of size.

74.1 The annual gathering of warships of Task Force 72 at Wentworth falls near Sydney Australia. (*Photo Michael Brown*)

74.2 HMS Queen at the National Maritime Museum model maritime show.

74.3 Warships on their allocated missions at the annual Potteries Navy Day, UK.

75.1 USN carrier enthusiasts at Dortmund Model show Germany.

by UK modeller Dave Markham, can be seen demonstrating a working Sea King helicopter. This is made to rise and fall and at the same time have the main and tail rotors function driven by electric motors connected through the suspension tube leading to the helicopter fuselage. Another novel feature is the functioning elevator, which can be raised or lowered at will with or without the Harrier using a scissor jack system. The Harrier is moved to and from the elevator by a set of worm gears and threaded rods, **Photo 76.2**.

Radio Control equipment

Two channels would be adequate in providing rudder and motor control regardless of the number of motors, as a single ESC could control any number of motors as if they were a single motor, providing the total current does not exceed the rating of the ESC (Electronic Speed Control).

Independent motor control - Photo Series 77

Two-channel operation is limited when there is a need for full independent motor control especially when manoeuvring large models. It is generally accepted that a 4-channel unit is the minimum requirement. In **Photo 77.1**, the R/C transmitter on the left of the picture is 4 channels only whilst the set on the right is also 4channel but is expandable by adding either switches or slide controls or both. This type of R/C set is ideal for controlling multi-functional models. Both sets operate on the 40 Megahertz (MHz) band, which is reserved for surface model operation in the UK. Additionally, 27MHz can be used, but it is illegal to use 35MHz equipment for surface models (boats and cars).

75.2 Kaiserliche Marine Model Group with their impressive indoor working diorama featuring a 1:100 battleship SMS Bayern.

77.1 Basic R/C equipment but the system on the right can expand the number of channels to over 32 allowing plenty of working functions.

Maintenance tips

If the general installation of equipment is well thought through, then the prospect of having trouble free sailing is greatly improved. However there are a number of general tips for maintaining a model that should prove quite useful.

This may seem obvious but before bringing the model to the lake check out the electrics and the R/C equipment on the bench. If it's going to malfunction then you can be sure it will do it on the water. Problems can often be traced to faulty wiring particularly to the battery or to loose connections anywhere.

The capacity (or lack of capacity) of the batteries is a common source of problems and batteries always needs to be properly maintained. If the propulsion battery is a NiCad, then it's wise to discharge the cells individually after each day's sailing. This will help maintain the true capacity of the cells. A gel cell, a sealed lead-acid type as used in stand-by systems, should be kept on a stand by trickle-charge between each sailing session. This will ensure that the cells remain in peak condition for use.

Radio frequency crystals

It is fairly rare to encounter receiver problems but frequency problems are frequent. Check out the crystals to ensure that they are a matching pair. Manufacturers are now marketing radio equipment that can scan the frequency band and set the transmitter and receiver to a vacant spot frequency thus eliminating the need to change crystals.

There are more and more models using battery eliminators for the receiver power supply using the main drive battery to provide the power to the receiver, servos and ESC. It is even more critical that the power supply cells are fully charged and in good order (see above). ESCs are also more reliable than in the past but faulty or wrong connections to this piece of electronics can prove expensive. The moral is always read the installation instructions before making any connections.

Slipping couplings and loose propellers

Loose propellers or slipping couplings are often the preserve of new models. But this can happen at any time and if it is a cast, bespoke brass propeller, it can be costly if it is lost. To avoid this happening, check that the lock nut is tight. When tightening up propellers to shafts it's advisable to allow a little margin of "play" between the end bearing and the locking nut, so that when the motor is running the end bearings on the shaft or stuffing box takes up the play and not the motor bearing. This can help reduce load and save on motor wear and tear.

Mooring up - Photo Series 78

A useful method of allowing a model to remain on the water but secure and more importantly, accessible, is to use a simple dock. This is made up from a length of timber (approximately 4ft

76.1 Working features on this model of HMS Fearless include an independently operated LCVP landing craft

76.2 A working elevator on a 1:96 HMS Illustrious.

long by 4in wide) with polystyrene underneath to ensure better floatation and enabling better protection for the side of the hull and bilge keel, **Photo 78.1**.

Lubrication
Lubricating the shafts is good practice and can be done with light oil from a header tank such as a discarded Humbrol paint tin. This also ensures that water does not feed into the hull and keeps the shaft free, **Photo 78.2**.

Presentation for shows and exhibitions - Photo Series 79
Although working models are made for the water they are also put on display for competition, or more often, as part of a general display at a show or exhibition and quite rightly attract attention. For this the usual functional lakeside stand can be discarded in place of something more in keeping, such as the superb polished

mahogany stand for this award winning HMS Kite by Paul Freshney deserving of the occasion and surroundings of the Model Engineer Exhibition, **Photo 79.1**.

Steering and manoeuvring single and multi screw warship - Photo Series 80
Rudders
A simple method for the construction of rudders for model warships was covered in Chapter 5. Apart from other types of devices for giving directional control the rudder mounted under the stern remains the most common method by which a ship is steered.

There are two basic types of rudders, balanced and unbalanced. A balanced rudder is one that pivots on its central axis in order to distribute the thrust of the water on its surface and as such makes steering of the ship easier because the centre of pressure on the rudder is brought nearer the axis. **Photo 80.1** shows an early example of the balanced rudder fitted to a builder's model

78.1 Useful method of mooring up a model keeps the model at a safe distance but remaining on the water.

76.2 A header tank, for lubricating shafts, made from a discarded paint tin.

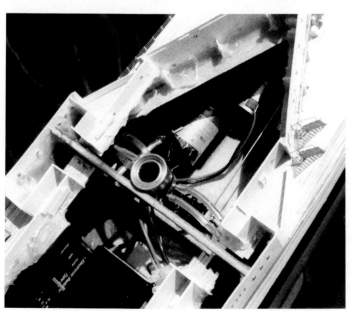

79.1 A superb HMS Kite. A flat iron gunboat entered into the Model Engineer Exhibition.

of the armoured cruiser HMS Amphitrite.

By contrast the unbalanced rudder is hinged at the leading edge and as such the forces required to turn the rudder are greater than those of a balanced rudder. Such a rudder is shown in **Photo 80.2** as fitted to the builder's model of the pre-

80.1 A balanced rudder fitted to a 1:48 builder model of the armoured cruiser HMS Amphitrite. *(Photo by kind permission of the Dock Museum Barrow in Furness)*

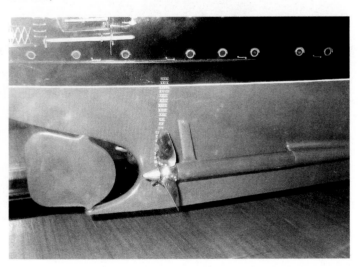

80.2 the battleship HMS Vengeance with an unbalanced rudder *(Photo by kind permission of the Dock Museum Barrow in Furness)*

81.1 A 1:96 HMS Iron Duke steering exceptionally well using a combination of rudder and 4 shafts.

dreadnought battleship HMS Vengeance.

Having twin rudders improves steering considerably and it is generally considered that a short ship is "handier" than a long ship. A good example of this in model form would be the twin shaft HMS Bulldog, even without independent motor control the model responds very positively to the rudders.

Thoughts on manoeuvring models

It is well to think of the model as a full-size vessel as the responses to the rudder will be similar. However the time frame for action and reaction on a model can be very much shorter. This is particularly noticeable if a model with a narrow beam to length (fineness) ratio is put into a continuous turn or circular pattern. The outward heeling tendency due to centrifugal force may be overcome by the inward heeling due to the rudder pressure. If the helm (transmitter rudder stick) were suddenly put fully over to the opposite, the inward heeling tendency due to the rudder would be suddenly removed. The model could respond by lurching precariously outwards. Under these conditions the rudder should be centred gradually so that as the rudder pressure is reduced, the model will return to upright trim. The usual maximum angle of the helm in ships of the RN is 35 degrees, although for models this may vary.

Steering with motors - Photo Series 81

Propellers can of course be used for steering. This is particularly useful in larger models where a rudder-only control gives a turn of larger radius than desired. This can be overcome and the radius of the turn greatly reduced if the motors are used in combination

with the rudders. For example the motor/motors on the side to which the helm is put would be worked ahead and the others astern. The revs applied to the individual motor would be a question of practice as all models/motor/rudder combinations have quite differing responses. Where there are up to four shafts and propellers, control should remain with a pair of motors as full independent control could prove difficult and expensive.

The 1:96 model of HMS Iron Duke, **Photo 81.1** is a good example this large model with quadruple shafts steers very easily using a combination of motors and rudders. Certainly, one of the most unusual warships ever to take to water must have been the Russian coastal defence ship Novgorod. She was propelled initially by no less than six propellers and can be seen here in model form at the Dortmund model show, **Photos 81.2**.

The worlds largest model or smallest aircraft carrier - Photo Series 82

The most appropriate picture to conclude this book has to be what could be considered one of the largest working models ever. This is Duncan Cameron's supremely impressive 28ft RO5 HMS Invincible, seen here being guided by tugs on it's departure from the annual Model Boat Convention at Ellesmere Port in the UK, **Photo 82.1**. Although to be fair this is not an R/C controlled model but controlled and operated from on board just like the real ship, but the question remains when is a model not a model or put another way when is a real ship a model?

Appendices

Appendix 1 Glossary

Warship class abbreviation

AGS Hydrographic Survey Ship RN

AK Cargo Ship USN

AKA Attack Cargo Ship USN

AH Hospital Ship

AO Tanker Oil

AOG Tanker Gasoline.

BB Battleship

CV Carrier

CVA Aircraft Carrier Attack

CVL Aircraft Carrier Light

CVE Aircraft Carrier Escort

CVF Aircraft Carrier Future

CVN Aircraft Carrier Nuclear USN

CA Cruiser heavy

CAG Cruiser Larger Guided Missile

CL Cruiser Light

CG Cruiser Guided Missile

CGN Cruiser Guided Missile Nuclear USN

CLGN Cruiser, Light Guided Missile, Nuclear. USN

DD Destroyer

DE Destroyer Escort

DDE Destroyer Converted to ASW fast escorts

DDG Destroyer Guided Missile

DLGN Frigate Guided Missile Nuclear. Discontinued

FF Frigate

FFG Frigate Guided Missile

MCM Mine Counter Measures

MCMV Mine Counter Measures Vessel

MCS Mine Counter Measures Support ship

LHA

LPH Landing Platform Helicopter

LPD Landing Platform Dock

LCC Amphibious Warfare Command ships

LSD Landing Ship Dock

LST Landing Ship Tank

LCU Landing Craft Utility

LCAC Landing Craft Air Cushion

LCM Landing Craft Mechanised

LCVP Landing Craft Vehicle & Personnel

LCV Landing Craft Vehicle

LCA Landing Craft Assault

OPV Offshore Patrol Vessel

RIB Rigid Inflatable Boat

RFA Royal Fleet Auxiliary

Appendix 2
Naval resource centres photographic archive / plans USN
National Archive, 8610 Adelphi Road, Collage Park,
MD 20740- 6001

Defence Visual Information Centre,
DVIC/OM-PA, 1363 Z Street Building 2730, March AFB,
CA 92518- 2727.
Tel (909) 413-2522. Fax 413- 2525

Naval War College Museum,
686 Cushing Road, Newport, RI 02841-1207
Tel (401) 841-4052/1317
www.nwc.navy.mil/default.htm

Mariners Museum Research Library,
100 Museum Drive, Newport News VA 23606-3759.
Tel (800) 581-7245
Photography Tel (757) 591-7767 or 7768
www.mariner.org/photo.html www.mariner.org/
travelingphoto.html

Smithsonian Institute
National Museum of American History,
Archive Centre. Room C-340,
Washington DC 20560 –0601
http://americanhistory.si.edu/csr/shipplan.htm

US Naval Institute Photographic Library,
118 Maryland Avenue, Annapolis, Maryland (410) 21402-5035
www.usni.org/hrp/hrp.html

US Naval Academy,
Nimitz Library Special Collection Division,
Annapolis, Maryland 21402-5029
Tel (410) 293-6912/613 Fax (410) 293-4926
e-mail creighto@nadn.navy.mil
Archives (410) 293-6917
e-mail lavalley@nadn.navy.mil

Commander Portsmouth Naval Shipyard,
Code 280.61 Portsmouth, New Hampshire 03804 –5000
Public Affairs fax (207)-438-1266
Historian (207)–438- 2565 or 2320

Naval Historical Centre,
Washington Navy Yard, 901 M Street Southeast, Washington
DC 20374 –5060
Tel (202) 433-2210 Fax (202) 433-3593
www.history.navy.mil

Photo Section Naval Historical Centre (CUP),
Building 108, 2nd Floor, Washington Navy Yard,
901 M Street Southeast ,Washington, DC 20374-5060
Tel (202) 433 2765
www.history.navy.mil/branches/nhcorg11.htm

Hampton Roads Naval Museum,
1 Waterside Drive, 248 Norfolk VA 23510-1607
Tel (757) 322-2987

Naval Resource Centres
Photographic Archive/ Plans UK/Europe
National Maritime Museum Picture Library, Greenwich,
London SE10 9NF
Tel 020 8312 6600/6704
www.nmm.ac.uk/picturelibrary

National Maritime Museum
Curator Historic Photographs and Ships Plans
Tel 020 8312 8600 Fax 020 8317`0263
Park Row, Greenwich, London SE10 9NF
e-mail plansandphotos@nmm.ac.uk
A huge collection of warship plans and photographs from
many periods up to the early post war years.

Imperial War Museum,
Department of Documents Lambeth Road SE1 6HZ
Tel 020 7416 5220
www.iwm.org.uk
A large collection of warship photographs WW1-2

National Archive,
Ruskin Avenue, Kew, Richmond, Surrey TW9 4DU
Tel 020 8392 5200
e-mail enquiry@nationalarchive.gov.uk
www.nationalarchives.gov.uk
War papers and official naval correspondence.

Dock Museum,
North Road, Barrow in Furness, Cumbria LA14 2PW
Tel 01229 894444
e-mail dockmuseum@barrowbc.gov.uk
Vickers photo archive 1870 –1960 some plans and a small
collection of quality Vickers built warship models.

Merseyside Maritime Museum,
Albert Dock, Liverpool L3 4AQ.
Tel 0151 4784499
Archive and Library. Holds the Bale collection of ship/
warship photographs

Discovery Museum Newcastle-upon-Tyne,
Blamford Square NE1 4JA
Tel 0191 232 6789 Fax 0191 230 2614
http://www.twmuseums.org.uk/discovery/turbinia.php
The original Turbinia and a fair collection of models of
warships built on the Tyne.

The Museum of Transport,
1 Bunhouse Road, Glasgow G3 8DP
e.mail Museums@cls.glasgow.gov.uk
http://www.clyde-valley.com/glasgow/transmus.htm
Holds the Clyde Room collection of Clyde built warships
models.

Mitchell Library, North Street, Glasgow G3 7DN
Tel 0141 287 2999 0r 2876
Some plans and photographs of Clyde built warships.

University of Glasgow Archive Service (Search Room),
13 Thurso Street, Glasgow G11 6PE
Tel for information and appointments 0141 3305515
Fax 0141 330 2640
e.mail dutyarch@archive.gla.ac.uk
Holds many warship plans including HMS Hood , HMAS
Australia, HMS Repulse and HMS Vanguard to name but a
few.

Royal Naval Museum Portsmouth,
Wright and Logan Collection of warship photographs.
http://www.wrightandlogan.co.uk/cart.php?target=category&
category_id=259

The Museum of Naval Firepower,
Priddy's Hard, Gosport, Hampshire PO12 4LE
Tel 023 9250 5600
e.mail info@explosion.org.uk
Naval Guns, plans /photos and many exhibits.

Fleet Air Arm Museum,
RNAS Yeovilton,Somerset BA22 8HT
Tel 01935 840565
www.fleetairarm.com
Records, photo archive and a number of carrier models

Musee de la Marine Paris
Palais de Chaillot, 17, Place du Trocadéro et du 11 Novembre,
75116 Paris.
http://www.cote.azur.fr/annuaire/site-musees-et-galeries-
musee-de-la-marine_82.htm
An excellent collection of plans/ photos of many French
warships from many periods.

Heeresgeschichtliches Museum,
Arsenal 3, Building 18, Vienna 1030, Austria
Tel 43 179 5610
e.mail bmlv.hgm@magnet.at
http://rubens.anu.edu.au/raid4/austria/vienna/museums/
heeresgeschichtliches/museum/ship_models/
Warship Models , plans and photo archive.

Useful Web addresses for photos & Plans

Photos
Navy News Stand (US Navy)
http://www.news.navy.mil/search/list.asp
Navy Photos (UK)
http://www.navyphotos.co.uk/index.htm
Sea Photo
http://www.warshipphotos.com/
Military Images.net
http://www.militaryimages.net/photopost/showgallery.
php/cat/511
Destroyer History Trust
http://www.destroyerhistory.org/
Nav Source (US Navy)
http://www.navsource.org/index2.htm
Atlantic Fleet Sales
http://www.atlanticfleetsales.com

Plans
Floating Drydock
http://floatingdrydock.com/
John Lambert Plans
http://www.lambert-plans.com/
Pacific Front
http://www.pacificfront.com/Plans.asp
Taubman Plans
(via Loyalhanna Dockyard) http://www.loyalhannadockyard.
com/
National Archives (USA via Maryland Silver Company)
http://www.marylandsilver.com/

Periodicals with a major warship content
Warship Conway Maritime Press
www.conwaymaritime.com frequency: annual.
The Naval Institute Guide to Combat Fleets
bi-annual
Warships International Fleet Review.
Monthly journal

Model magazines with a strong warship content
Model Shipwright:
UK Quarterly
Model Boats Magazine:
monthly Published by Encanta Media Ltd
e.mail modelboats@subscription.co.uk
or USA Canada info@wiseowlmagazines.com
Marine Modelling International:
monthly
Fine Scale Modeller

Appendix 3
Specialist Manufactures and Suppliers

Hulls
The Floating Drydock
P.O. Box 9587
Treasure Island, FL 33740 USA
Fax: 727 363 8198
email: drydock@floatingdrydock.com

Hulls, plans ,fittings, photos.
The Scale Shipyard
866 Orange Avenue, # 3 Long Beach CA 90805- 4146
Tel 562 428 5027 USA
Online Catalogue
http://scaleshipyard.com/catolog%20pages/index.html
An extensive range of warship hulls

Loyalhanna,
7527 Gilbert Road, Bergen, NY 14416
Tel 585 494 0027 USA
www.loyalhannadockyard.com
email LHDockyard@aol.com

Fleetscale Westward Mouldings Ltd
The New Factory, Greenhill, Delaware Road, Gunnislake,
Cornwall PL18 9AS Tel {+44} 1822832120
Fax {+44} 1822 833938
www.fleetscale.com

PS Ships/Sirmar
PO Box 369, St Helens, Merseyside WA10 9AU
Tel 01744 22337 UK
www.sirmarmodelships.com

Warship hulls, fittings
Metcalf Mouldings,
1 Wentworth Cottage, Haultworth Cottage, Dane End,
Ware SG11 1JG
Tel 01920 438686
Email metcalf.mouldings@virgin.net

Some warship hulls
Deans Marine,
Conquest Drive, Farcet,
Peterborough PE7 3DH
Tel 0044 1733 244166
www.deansmarine.co.uk
Many periods of warship also semi kits available

Cammett Ltd,
Adlen House, Eardisland, Leominster, HR6 9BD
Tel 01544 388514 e-mail
cammettco@btinternet.com
www.cammett.co.uk
Post-war RN 1:96 Hulls and fittings

Propellers, shafts and "A" frames
George Sitek,
1Halton Drive, Crewe, Cheshire CW2 8TA
Tel 01270- 251643
www.gsitek-props.co.uk
email office@gsitek.props.co.uk

Propellers, shafts and "A" frames
Propellers
The Prop Shop,
Unit 5, Alscot Park Stables, Preston-on-Stour,
Warwickshire CV37 BBL
email simon@prop-shop.co.uk
Cast propellers

Ships' boats
Quaycraft,
73 Chambercombe Road, Ilfracombe, N, Devon.
EX34 9PH Tel 01271 866837
Ships for boats for many scales and navies

Timber
Modelling Timber Co.,
65 St Lawrence Avenue, Snaith, East Yorkshire DN14 9JH
Tel 01405 861734
Many different types of timber for the model boat builder

Specialist Paints
White Ensign Models, South Farm, Snitton, Ludlow,
Shropshire
SY8 3EZ UK
www.WhiteEnsignModels.com
e-mail wem@onetel.com

References

Ships and Aircraft of the US Fleets 13th Edition
Norman Polmar, *Arms and Armour Press.*

Naval Institute Guide to Combat Fleets of the World 2005-2006 Eric Wertheim, *Naval Institute Press*

Naval Institute Guide to World Naval Weapons Systems 1997-1998
Norman Friedheim, *Naval Institute Press*

Surface Warships Volume 3
Dr PJ Gates, *Brassey Sea Power*

Soviet Warships
John Jorden, *Arms and Armour Press.*

Guide to the Soviet Navy 2nd Edition
Breyer and Polmar

Slava, Udaloy and Sovremennyy
Steven J Zaloga *Concord Publications*

British, Soviet, French, Dutch Battleships of WW2
William H Garzke Jr & Robert O Dunlin

US Cruisers an Illustrated Design History
Norman Friedman *Arms and Armour Press*

The Worlds Warships
Raymond VB Blackman *Macdonald & Co Ltd*

US Destroyers an Illustrated Design History
Norman Friedman *Naval Institute Press*

Battleships - United States Battleships in World War II
Robert O Dunlin Jnr William H Garzke Jnr.
Naval Institute Press

Die AtomKreuzer der US Navy
Wilhelm M Donko *Bechtermunz Verlag*

Conway's All the Worlds Fighting Ships 1947-1995

Naval Weapons of World War II
John Campbell *Conway Maritime Press.*

British Navy Destroyers Since 1945
Leo Marriott *Ian Allan Ltd.*

Royal Navy Frigates 1945–1983
Leo Marriott *Ian Allan Ltd.*

US Warships of WW2
Paul H Silverstone *Ian Allan Ltd*

United States Warship Camouflage 1939-1945
Chris Ellis *Pique Publications*
Naval Camouflage 1914- 1945 - A Complete Visual Reference
David Williams *Chatham Publishing*

Royal Navy Camouflage 1939–1945
Peter Hodges *Almark Publishing*

Ship Models Their Purpose and Development from 1650 to the present
Brian Lavery and Simon Stephens *National Maritime Museum*

Ship Yard Practice As Applied to Warship Construction
NJ McDermaid. *Longman Green 1911.*

Manual of Seamanship 1909; 1915; 1930; 1937; 1951; 1965; 1975 *Royal Navy*

Jane's Dictionary of Naval Terms
Compiled by Joseph Palmer

Practical Construction of Warships
RN Newton *Longman Green 1949*

Warships of World War II
HT Lenton & JJ Colledge *Ian Allan*

British Warships since 1945 - Part 5 Frigates
Mike Critchley *Maritime Books*